"Orville Rogers' greatest accomplishments are not his amazing U.S. World Indoor and Outdoor Track records in the 90-99 age group, or his numerous mission trips, but his ability to inspire and motivate people to 'continue the race.'"
—DR. ROBERT JEFFRESS, SENIOR PASTOR, FIRST BAPTIST CHURCH, DALLAS, TEXAS

"If you believe God can use you in ways beyond your imagination, the story of Orville Rogers will attest to the fact that anything is possible. *The Running Man* is a story about a remarkable man who trusted God and committed his life serving Jesus Christ. In a world of fake heroes and here-to-day-gone-tomorrow people, God has used Orville's life story as a testimony to faith, perseverance, and love."
—WOODY MCLENDON, PRESIDENT, JAARS, INC.

"Wrapped in a small Cessna airplane, surrounded by enough fuel torch a small city, I watched him take off to fly that plane over the Pacific without companion. As he took off, I said to myself, 'There is a remarkable pilot, an amazing missionary, and courageous visionary!' His story needs to be told. Here it is, *The Running Man*. Don't miss a syllable of this inspiring story of humble service to our Lord."
—PAIGE PATTERSON, PRESIDENT, SOUTHWESTERN BAPTIST THEOLOGICAL SEMINARY, FORT WORTH, TEXAS

"Orville Rogers' commitment to an unwavering steward-ship of life makes me even more willing to leverage all of my time, talent, and treasure for God's glory! Through his gener-osity I better understand what biblical munificence looks like.
—TODD PETERSON, CHAIRMAN, PRO ATHLETES
OUTREACH; CHAIRMAN EMERITUS OF SEED
COMPANY

"Orville Rogers' life is a great encouragement to everyone who knows him. He is a remarkable man, friend, and brother in Christ. His story will move you and get you moving!"
—DR. ROY PETERSON, PRESIDENT & CEO,
AMERICAN BIBLE SOCIETY

"God accomplishes history through men. There are many *firsts* in history described in this book, and Orville has been an instrument in participating with God in these *firsts*."
—SAMUEL CHIANG, PRESIDENT AND CEO, THE
SEED COMPANY

"Orville Rogers has been an inspiration to so many of us who desire to serve the Lord even into old age. He reminds me of Caleb, who said, 'Now, here I am this day, eighty-five years old. As yet I am as strong this day as on the day that Moses sent me; just as my strength was then, so now is my strength for war, both for going out and for coming in. Now therefore, give me this mountain of which the Lord spoke in that day' (Joshua 14:10b–12a). Orville has claimed his 'mountain' and he has inspired us all."
—GARY COOK, CHANCELLOR, DALLAS BAPTIST
UNIVERSITY

"After my wife's death Orville came up for a visit. What agenda would compel a ninety-eight-year-old man to drive from Dallas to Oklahoma City? It took me a while to discover it. His agenda was . . . me! Once again, Orville was at his best, giving counsel, love, encouragement, and the assurance that, by God's grace, any of us can make it through the tests of life. Yes! We can!"

—Tom Elliff, President Emeritus,
International Mission Board, SBC

"Orville Rogers has been a cherished friend for over forty years. I first met him and Esther Beth when he was a Braniff Airline pilot back in the 70s. We became instant friends. He is one of the finest Christian gentlemen I have ever met. After his Braniff days he became a pilot flying supplies, equipment, and people to hard-to-reach places around the world on difficult missionary efforts. He has served as deacon and leader in his church. His passion for God compels him to keep going as he nears one hundred years old. He is a world class athlete, as is easily seen from the competitive races he has run for decades, and he still leads his age group in every race. These pages will introduce you to one of the truly unique and most incredible man I have ever met."

—Jimmy Draper, President Emeritus, LifeWay

"One of Orville's great sayings is 'You are only young once, but you can be immature for a lifetime.' I have referenced his quote hundreds of times through the years. I hope readers will enjoy meeting one of the greatest friends God has given me. I love the man like a brother."

—Bernie May, Founder, The Seed Company

"Whenever I think of Orville, I remember something he said years ago that has stuck with me. "No matter how thin the pancake, there are always two sides."
—RAYMOND R. BERRY, PRESIDENT, INTELLIGENT TECHNOLOGY, INC.; FORMER BOARD MEMBER, JAARS

"Early one summer morning in 1975, Orville Rogers and Bob Burdick fired up the Aero Commander's engines at the Charlotte, North Carolina, airport. As my fiancé and I stood alone waving from a nearby slope, I knew where they would end up—way across the ocean in my home country. They were not going for financial gain but to help facilitate the spread of the gospel through Bible translation work. This plane was going to bring food to the hungry, transport the sick, and carry the Word of God to the heart languages tucked away in remote regions of the Philippines. Orville Rogers ran the race using his time, talent, and resources to accomplish God's purposes in light of eternity! What a legacy to follow!

This is from my heart to the man God has placed in my life as a mentor, encourager, and faithful prayer and financial partner, and I am truly humbled to have him ask me to write a little bit on his book."
—NARD PUGYAO, JAARS PILOT

THE
RUNNING
MAN

Flying High for the Glory of God

ORVILLE ROGERS

Clovercroft Publishing

The Running Man: Flying High for the Glory of God

©2016 by Orville Rogers

Published by Clovercroft Publishing, Franklin, Tennessee

Published in association with Larry Carpenter of Christian Book Services, LLC.

Cover Design by Omar Mediano

Interior Design by Suzanne Lawing

Edited by Gail Fallen

Printed in the United States of America

978-1-942557-90-6

DEDICATION

To Esther Beth (also known as E.B. and, her favorite, Beth). She was my companion for seventy years as friend, prayermate, lover and wife, mother of our children, and Grand Mom to many more. Without complaint she managed the home and guided the children while I was away so many times on trips for my employer Braniff Airways, or on missionary ferry flights for Wycliffe Bible Translators or the Southern Baptist International Mission Board. Her children "rise and call her blessed. Her husband also praises her: Many women are capable, but you surpass them all!" (Proverbs 31:28–29).

To my children, grandchildren, and great-grandchildren, who have provided me with joy and thanksgiving to God for their beautiful lives and their dedication to God.

ACKNOWLEDGMENTS

Many people helped make this book happen, but at the top of the list is my friend and publicist Cindy Birne, whose enthusiasm and tremendous support throughout the process has made this journey a great adventure.

I am grateful to the many friends who offered to write words of introduction or commendation for this book, including Dr. Kenneth Cooper, MD, MPH; Dr. Robert Jeffress; Woody McClendon; Paige Patterson; Dr. Roy Peterson; Todd Peterson; Samuel Chiang; Bernie May; Raymond R. Berry; Tom Elliff; Gary Cook; and Nard Pugyao. A special thanks to Risë Corn and Roger Adamson for encouraging me to pen my life story and for introducing me to Cindy Birne. I wish to express my sincere gratitude to writer Barbara Norris, without whom this book would not be possible, and to my creative cover designer, Omar Mediano, for capturing the essence of my life story. I also want to thank my publisher, Larry Carpenter, president and CEO of Christian Book Services, LLC, and Clovercroft Publishing for his help and guidance throughout the publishing process.

Finally, I want to thank the many medical professionals who have rescued me from serious medical issues and kept me running for the prize from God: "Well done, thou good and faithful servant" (Matthew 25:21).

I hope to inspire all the readers of this book that all can know the Lord Jesus as Savior and Lord, and can faithfully serve Him all the days of their lives.

FOREWORD

Mr. Orville Rogers told me that at age fifty, he picked up a copy of my book *Aerobics*, which led him to begin a jogging program. I did not have a chance to work with him until he came for his first comprehensive medical examination on October 15, 1971.

Since that time he has been a faithful participant as a member of our Cooper Center Longitudinal Study, in which we are trying to show that regular physical activity can reduce deaths from all causes and prolong lives. Of the 120,000 patients we have seen at the Cooper Clinic since December 1970, he is truly our "poster boy" for showing that life can be full, active, and rewarding if you adhere to the lifestyle we recommend to our patients who come to our clinic. This does include proper weight, proper diet, proper exercise, proper supplementation, and having an annual comprehensive medical evaluation.

It was in 1993, after many years of running and having worked up to a twenty-six-mile marathon, that Orville began to notice a decrease in his performance. At first he thought it may have been some type of allergic response since he seemed to be getting more short of breath. For a while I had him run on an indoor track to see if preventing exposures to allergens in the outdoor air would help, but it didn't. During that time, I continued to monitor his stress electrocardiogram and the results were surprisingly normal, indicative of an outstanding and highly conditioned athlete. But then, in 1993, his electrocardiogram suddenly developed changes that were clearly abnormal. This was followed up with a coronary arteriogram and a six-vessel coronary bypass procedure.

During his ninetieth year (2008), we did a CT angiogram

to see if the bypass grafts were still patent. It had been fifteen years since his surgery (and ordinarily, a graft remain opens for a maximum of seven years), and his vessels were all widely patent. Even at the time of his last complete examination at the Cooper Clinic on December 21, 2015, his stress electrocardiogram showed no signs of any coronary artery obstruction and, for that reason, he has been able to safely continue with his competitive athletics.

As stress testing has been used at the Cooper Clinic, we have developed age-group classifications for fitness based on the length of time a patient can walk on the treadmill. For several decades, Orville has continued to set age group records for men, and now holds those records for men eight-five to eighty-nine years of age, ninety to ninety-four years of age, and ninety-five to ninety-nine years of age! His performance continues to keep him in the "impossible" range of fitness for men in his age group, and that is why he holds sixteen age-group world records for individual and relay events!

Orville is a deeply committed Christian who has gained some notoriety for ferrying single engine aircraft to missionaries all over the world. On one occasion he was delivering a single engine airplane to missionaries in New Guinea, and the first leg of his flight was from California to Hawaii. It took seventeen hours to travel that leg due to carrying extra fuel that tended to overload the aircraft. He always had to check the weather conditions before departing (and his wife, Esther Beth, always traveled with him), since if he encountered severe turbulence, he said there was a possibility that the "wings could flop off"! Fortunately, with his flights all over the world—not only to the Far East but to Africa—he gives credit to the Lord for always allowing him to fly in good weather, never encountering any extreme emergencies.

In their 60s, Orville and Esther Beth, on a Christian mission to Africa, both climbed Mount Kilimanjaro in Tanzania;

Esther Beth reached 15,400 feet while Orville made it to the summit, at an altitude of over 19,000 feet!

My wife once said to me that both Esther Beth and Orville are such outstanding Christians that when they disappear and we are still left, "the rapture must have come" and we didn't make it!

Through Orville's career as a Braniff Airlines captain, he and some other commercial airline pilots invested in oil and gas properties. It just so happened that those properties are located in the midst of the Barnett Shale deposits which has enabled him to be extraordinarily wealthy and extremely generous in supporting not only a variety of church and Christian-related activities, but also The Cooper Institute. Not only has he contributed immense data to our Cooper Center Longitudinal Study as a patient but also he continues to support our research with his ongoing financial commitments.

In conclusion, I would say that Orville Rogers is truly one of the most deeply committed, disciplined, and talented individuals I have ever had the privilege of working with in my sixty years of practicing medicine. I only hope that one day when I "grow up," I will be able to enjoy the highest quality of life which he has been able to enjoy. And I am sure that when the day comes for him to join friends and other family members in heaven, our Lord will say, "Well done, thou good and faithful servant!"

Kenneth H. Cooper, MD, MPH
April 17, 2016

CONTENTS

PROLOGUE

Any pilot who straps a single-engine airplane on his back and flies across the Atlantic or Pacific even one time, much less twelve times, as I did, is bold. Writing these lines at age ninety-eight, I respectfully disagree with E. Hamilton Lee, who coined the adage, there are old pilots and bold pilots but no old, bold pilots. Without question, I am an old, bold pilot.

I am also "The Running Man." I began to set world records at age ninety, which garnered a fair amount of attention. Plenty of people are probably surprised to see me on the track instead of shuffling around with a walker. They don't know I'm an old, bold pilot accustomed to pushing the limits, embracing the challenges, taking chances (which I prefer to call calculated risks), and moving forward when I am expected to stand still.

In the summer of 1927, Charles Lindbergh flew the Spirit of St. Louis in a circle above our little schoolhouse in Oklahoma. That brush with greatness inspired me at an early age to reach for the heights and ignore the consequences.

The first time I went up in an airplane, at age eleven, I took a chance on a barnstormer who came to our town. My mother might have been worried about kidnapping or a crash landing, but I gave the stranger with the flying machine every penny in my piggy bank for a fifteen-minute ride. Even at that young age, I had faith that God watched over me and wouldn't let me make a choice I would regret.

I deviated from the expected path when I chose to pursue a career in the service of our Lord. With a passion for flying and a degree in engineering, my family assumed I would either become a pilot or join my uncles in the oil and gas business. But prayer and my instincts told me to attend a seminary and prepare for a position with the church. I took a chance on serving God, and He repaid me with a better, richer life than I could ever have imagined.

When I instructed pilots during World War II and prepared them to fly in defense of our country, I had to push the limits of my endurance nearly every day. Working incredibly long hours, we had to take risks and break rules to churn out enough pilots to beat Hitler and the Japanese.

Under these dire circumstances and others, I calculated the risks and took them. I brought a great deal of knowledge and experience into the cockpit when I flew small aircraft all over the world for JAARS (Jungle Aviation and Radio Service). Whenever I took off from Honolulu flying a small airplane across the Pacific headed for tiny islands like Majuro or Tarawa, I faced fifteen or more hours of flying time. I knew the limits of my body and mind. I knew the weather and upper-wind predictions. When I was greatly overloaded by special ferry permit, I knew the limits of airspeed and how far my airplane could go with the fuel on board. I am no fool, and I do not have a death wish. Taking all the factors into consideration, I was more than willing to accept the calculated risks involved in the delivery of missionary planes to be used in the service of my Lord.

I embraced the challenge when I fell in love with a young woman before she fell in love with me. Esther Beth Shannon and I became friends when we were both still teenagers at the University of Oklahoma. She had a boyfriend at the time, but I sensed he would not last long. Instead of playing by the rules, moving on, and finding somebody else, I took a chance on her and waited patiently. She eventually came around. We were married for sixty-four years, nine months, and five days. Though she has passed away, we will continue to be soul mates forever, and I will see her again in heaven.

When Beth and I had our first child, I knew very little about being a father. Mine left us when I was six years old, and our stern and unaffectionate grandfather raised my sister and me. Those two men were the only models I had, but I didn't settle for being a fatherless child. At age ten, I chose a different kind of father: my heavenly Father. He taught me all I know about loving and guiding the family Beth and I made together.

Calculating risk was the name of the game when I invested in the oil and gas business and the stock market. Instead of going with the herd, I followed my instinct for boldness and rode out the cycles of boom and bust that scare off more timid investors. In another contrarian move, I gave away most of the money I made in my lifetime, preferring to put it to work for God, the source of all abundance.

Abundant good health and a competitive spirit keep me running races even though my competitors have quit. When my wife passed away two weeks before my first national championship meet, I kept running. She wouldn't have wanted me to quit. When a stroke paralyzed me on the third anniversary of her death, I devoted myself to rehab, and within weeks, I was running. Nowadays, when my body starts aching and my knees threaten to buckle, I keep running. Stopping would mean going home and plopping myself on a recliner. That's not for me. I'm the running man.

My Lord Jesus said He came so that we might have abundant life. I believe my willingness to take chances creates the abundance Jesus promised. I have lived to the fullest, with gusto, and I don't intend to stop until I pass the finish line—running.

RUNNING FOR MY LIFE

From the time I saw the first airplane fly over my house on the great plains of Oklahoma until the last time I climbed out of a cockpit at age seventy-nine, my passion was flying. Now, at age ninety-eight, I have gained more notoriety for my running than for flying airplanes. As one of the oldest competitors in the world, I am an object of curiosity and a source of inspiration.

When they see me run, people assume I must be quite passionate about it. Why else keep running when almost everyone else my age is either dead or reclining in front of a TV? I keep running and competing for three reasons:

First, it keeps me active, and that keeps me alive. As Dr. Kenneth Cooper outlined so eloquently in his first book, *Aerobics*, longevity and quality of life are directly related to a life-long pursuit of physical fitness—aerobic activity specifically. That's how and why I came to running in the first place.

Second, I run competitively because I like to win. It's that simple. Breaking world records is extremely satisfying, and it provides a goal to work toward. I think goal setting contributes to longevity, too. I want to compete in some field events when I am one hundred years old. That's a goal that will keep me active for the next couple of years.

Third, and most important, running gives me a platform. Through running, I create opportunities to talk about God. I've been interviewed numerous times on local and national television. I've been featured in newspapers and magazines countless times. I don't seek out this publicity for myself. I do it to get out my message about God's love. Though I try to get in a Christian testimony when I'm being interviewed, the quotes don't always get into print or video, and that's okay. The journalists have their job to do, and they want to do it the best they know how. This book, on the other hand, is mine, and I get to choose what goes in it. For me, it is another opportunity to witness, and if it helps and inspires people who want to remain physically fit in their later years, all the better.

* * *

The moment I decided to start running is still vivid in my mind. It was May 1968, and I was fifty years old. I was flying Dallas-Chicago trips for Braniff. On a layover, I went to a Chicago hotel coffee shop for breakfast. There weren't any newspapers to read, so I looked at the bookrack in the lobby. One book stood out. It was titled *aerobics*, all lowercase, which was a little odd. I recognized the word from biology class, but instead of an illustration of mitochondria and electron-transport chains, this book's cover featured a bicycler and a jogger. I picked it up and read the lines above the title: "The most effective physical fitness plan ever!" The author was Kenneth H. Cooper, MD; MPH; Major, USAF Medical Corps. A fellow

Air Force guy! I had to read it.

Over breakfast, I dove into the book and finished that day. Dr. Cooper had researched physical fitness in the Air Force and translated his findings into ideas about exercise for the general public. I didn't know then—and he didn't either—that this book would play a major role in kicking off a worldwide running revolution. I read it cover to cover, and the next day I started running.

The fitness program Dr. Cooper outlined in that book motivated me, and I committed myself to it immediately. That commitment, and my subsequent involvement with Dr. Cooper, continue to this day, some forty-eight years later.

As a ninety-eight-year-old competitive runner and forty-eight-year devotee of Dr. Cooper's fitness regimen, I am living proof that he's on to something. I am not just living longer thanks to aerobics, I am living better. I am a happy man. I enjoy life as my Creator intended, and I am enthusiastic about the future. You can't ask for more than that.

From Keds to Nikes

Running shoes hadn't been invented back in 1968, when I first started running. I ran in Keds. They were just sneakers, and they didn't offer any padding or support. Then Adidas came out with the first shoes specifically made for running. Nike's research teams were working on their own designs at the same time, and eventually they came up with a far superior shoe. In fact, the improvement in today's Nikes over Adidas is greater than the advances the Adidas offered over Keds. I wouldn't consider running in anything but Nikes, and that's not just because they're a great shoe. It turns out, my connection to the world's greatest running shoe runs deeper than I could ever have imagined.

The Phone Call

By the time I reached the age of ninety-seven, I thought I had experienced every life-changing event God had in store for me. Naturally, He had other ideas. I was working at my computer one fine spring day in 2014 when I received a phone call. A pleasant but unfamiliar voice came on the line. "My name is Sandra Rogers Weible," she said, "and I am your sister."

I have a strong heart, but that news left it pounding. I hadn't heard anything having to do with my father for ninety years. Gazing out my window over the tops of the budding oaks and pecans, I thought about the man who gave me my last name and nothing more.

* * *

A few months after that first phone call from my newfound sister, I traveled to Bend, Oregon, to meet her. She and her husband, the late Vern, live out in the country. The nearest neighbors are a half mile or so away.

Bend is not on the rainy Oregon coast. It's inland, east of the Cascades, so it's fairly arid, like West Texas if West Texas had pine trees. Nevertheless, Sandra has made a lovely garden. She grows flowers and raises some vegetables in the spring, before the dry summers set in.

Sandra and Vern are friendly, down-to-earth people, and, like me, they're believers. So we hit it off. Sandra is a little more outgoing than I am. I still have problems with that, although I've tried to improve since Beth died. When we first connected, Sandra would talk on the phone with me for an hour or more. We wanted to know all about each other. Now that we've pretty much caught up, the conversations are shorter, but we stay in close touch.

The first night I was in Portland, we went out to dinner

with Sandra's sons, John and Jeb, her daughter Julie, and Julie's husband, Tom Clarke. This is where the story gets even stranger. Remember, I'm a competitive runner, and I'm crazy about Nike shoes. Well, Tom Clarke served as president of Nike from 1994 to 2000. Now he is president of innovation for Nike. What are the odds?

The next morning, I visited with Tom at the Nike headquarters in Beaverton, which is just a few miles west of downtown Portland. In the two or three hours we spent together, he showed me around their beautiful, 270-acre campus. It's heavily wooded, with pine trees and grassy areas and a running trail that meanders past thirty-eight buildings. For a running nut like me, getting squired around the world headquarters of Nike by one of the guys who made the company successful was quite a thrill.

Tom introduced me to Phil Knight, who was president of Nike at the time. He told me the story of Nike's first running shoe. Thinking they could develop something better than the old Keds or Converse, their first trial involved a piece of rubber and a waffle iron to create a revolutionary sole designed just for runners. I saw the waffle iron. It's still on display.

I left Nike headquarters with a bag of gifts, including a pair of their latest shoes. You can imagine I wouldn't dream of wearing anything else.

Touring Nike headquarters was a lot of fun for me, but nothing compares to the deep satisfaction I gained in finding a sister I never knew I had and learning, at last, what became of the man who left my mother, my sister, and me ninety-two years ago.

OKLAHOMA BOYHOOD

A Prophetic Christening

My name is Orville Curtis Rogers. My mother named me after Orville Wright, and I am surmising that she thought Curtis Wright was Orville's brother, though everyone knows his name was Wilbur. Curtis Wright tinkered with designing airplanes too. He tried to duplicate Orville and Wilbur's success, but he built an airplane that didn't fly. I don't mind being named Curtis. I just want to be sure everyone knows I wasn't named after that guy. I don't know why my mother had such a strong interest in flying, but she must have. Why else would she have named me after one of the fathers of flight?

My People

My mother's name was Lily Leona Johnston, though sometimes I saw it spelled Lillie. She met my father, Stephen Rogers, in Hubbard, Texas, a small town southeast of Dallas in Hill County. It was organized when the railroads came through back in the late 1800s, and it came to be known as a health resort when healing mineral waters were discovered there.

I think both sides of my family are Anglo-Saxon with some Scottish thrown in. One of my grandsons traced my mother's line back to the 1500s in England. Sandra told me that on my dad's side, we were descendants of King Robert the Bruce of Scotland, who ruled from 1306 to 1329. I don't have proof of that, but Sandra insists it's true.

My dad's father was a Baptist minister, probably in Hubbard, though I'm not sure about that. My mother told me her father-in-law was a good preacher, but you needed to keep an eye on him around the women folk. That still makes me chuckle.

I was born on November 28, 1917, at home in my parents' ranch house near Hubbard. The house was moved at some point to the Hubbard town square as part of a display of pioneer life. Years later, when I went back to see it, I found out it had been completely demolished in a fire.

My Dad

My parents and I moved to Okemah in central Oklahoma soon after I was born. The town was named after a Kickapoo Indian chief who set up camp there in anticipation of the opening of the town site in 1902. Okemah sits on prairie land that once was home to the Osage and Quapaw until they ceded the land to the US in 1825. Later the area was assigned to the Creek Nation.

When we arrived in Okemah in 1918, there were still quite a few Native Americans living there, but the town's big claim to fame is Woody Guthrie, who was born there in 1912. That would make him five years old when I got to town, and he didn't leave until 1928 or thereabouts, so we probably crossed paths without my knowing it. Astronaut and test pilot William Reid Pogue was born there in 1930. I have to think he had some of the same feelings I did when he looked across that prairie land and up at the endless blue sky. Woody Guthrie hopped a train, and William Pogue and I took to the sky, all of us looking for our futures beyond that wide horizon.

* * *

My earliest remembrance, at age four, is the day my sister Veva was born. My mother delivered her at home, which was the norm in those days. I was shuttled off in the corner somewhere, but I still remember the excitement in the air. I imagine the midwife came to help, and my dad was likely taking orders from her when he wasn't pacing, listening to my mother's moans and cries.

The few memories I have of my dad are hazy, but those events I do remember must have made quite an impression. For instance, I still remember the day he came home with a broken toe from his job at an icehouse. He had mishandled a cake of ice and it fell on his foot. That crippled him up for a while.

We lived briefly in Oklahoma City, and one of my first run-ins with Dad took place in the backyard of our house there. Dad had told me not to climb the trees. Of course, I went ahead and climbed the biggest and best, the one with a nice fat limb to sit on, where I could survey the whole neighborhood. I slipped and fell onto the bare, hard ground. Through my tears, I saw him dash down the back steps and run to me. I thought he was going to help me, but instead he yanked me up and spanked me. I'll tell you what, I never crossed him again. I didn't resent him for that spanking. I knew I was guilty, but

I thought, *why is he spanking me when I'm already hurt?* Then, when I saw it from his perspective, I realized I'd disobeyed him and I deserved to be punished. I guess that was one lesson my dad imparted to me.

Soon after that incident, he moved us to Edmond, Oklahoma. It's a suburb of Oklahoma City now, but when we moved there in 1923, it was still a small town that grew up around the Santa Fe railroad. I imagine we left Oklahoma City because my father couldn't pay the rent. Whatever the reason, the move to Edmond didn't solve his problems or cure his tendency to drift.

After we'd been there about three months, he took off for good. I don't think he even left a note. He just disappeared. At the time, I didn't have any animosity or hard feelings. He was just gone, and I didn't care. It was not until I realized many years later what his leaving had done to my mother that I developed some very definite feelings about him, and they weren't good. I was six years old when he left us, and I never heard from him again.

One night, shortly after he left, I was tearing through our backyard, not looking where I was going. I didn't see a low-hanging clothesline stretched across my path, and I caught it right under my chin. It flipped me back hard and knocked the wind out of me. My back ached and my head pounded, but the good news was, this time, Dad wasn't around to spank me. For a little guy like me, losing my dad was something like that clothesline. His leaving knocked me for a loop. I just didn't know it at the time.

* * *

Ninety years later, when Sandra called me out of the blue, I finally learned what happened to my dad.

"What can you tell me about our father?" I asked Sandra

during that first phone call.

"Almost nothing," she said. "My mother kicked him out when I was almost three because he was a drunkard." She told me he was a salesman by trade. Apparently a pretty good one when he was sober. But he couldn't hold a job for very long, and he became a drifter. He had botched his life with us in Oklahoma, and he hadn't fared any better out West.

When I visited Sandra in Bend, she showed me our father's death certificate. He died in a Los Angeles flophouse, literally dead drunk. That's not a very pretty picture, but it's the truth.

A New Home

After my dad left, my mother took us back to Okemah to live with her parents, Reuben and Mary Johnston. All my mother's folks were country people, including my granddad, who was a dirt farmer. He and Grandmother had moved from Gadsden, Alabama, around 1914 and bought a small farm about two-and-a-half miles east of town.

Granddad was the boss of the family, which meant my mother had little say over how I was raised. That was Granddad's job. He was very strict and domineering. In all my years growing up in his house, I never got any words of praise from him, only criticism. That was their way of life, and I came to realize that had to be okay.

I knew they loved me, though neither my mother nor my grandparents ever told me so. They just weren't very affectionate. My mom and my grandmother would hug me once in a while, but I never saw my granddad kiss or hug my grandmother in all the time I lived with them.

The nearest Granddad ever came to complimenting my mom (that I know of) was one day when he invited two or three of his croquet buddies to come for a lunch my mom had prepared. When the men complimented the cooking, Granddad said, "Yes, Lilly can set a pretty good table when she sets her mind to it." You can imagine how unusual that was if I still remember it to this day. That was just his way.

Granddad worked about two hundred acres. Part of it was pastureland that we kept for three milk cows, a couple of mules, and a few horses, which I took care of. We didn't buy much food for them. They just ate what they could forage in the pasture, and we grew oats for extra feed. I loved riding bareback on our old gray mare, and I had a collie that went everywhere with me.

For first and second grade, I walked to the country school about a mile from where we lived. It was a one-room, three-grade school with one teacher. For third grade, I took the bus to a regular school in town.

I am by nature or by choice very inquisitive. I always wanted to know what was going on, what made things tick, and that kept me busy. I built several model airplanes and fooled around with electric motors and that sort of thing.

All that busyness kept my focus off personal relationships. I didn't really pay much attention to other people like I should have. It's no wonder, considering the way I was brought up, without much in the way of close family relationships. I had to get outside of my family to develop any closeness with anybody, and I did make friends, but it wasn't easy.

The Johnston Uncles

My mother had four living brothers and one who died at the age of twenty. They were a pretty close-knit family. Uncle Bill in Oklahoma City married late and never had any children. Uncle Ralph in Houston also married late. They adopted a boy and a girl. Uncle Daniel lived in Clarksville, Arkansas, and had four boys. Another brother, Votie, out in West Texas, had two daughters.

We went to visit Uncle Votie several times in the touring car my granddad bought after we moved in with him. That's when he learned to drive—not very well, I should add. One time, he had a little too much speed coming up against a fence. He was jamming on the brakes and pulling back on his steering wheel, yelling, "Whoa! Whoa! Whoa!" as if he was reining in a wild stallion. We hit the fence—not hard enough to cause much damage, except to his pride.

The car had isinglass windows set into canvas that we snapped up when it rained or turned cold. There were four seats, maybe five—two in the front and three in the back—and running boards. Those came in handy when we went on trips. There wasn't much room in the car, so we stowed our bags on the running boards.

Loaded down like that, we visited our relatives in West Texas looking like the Okies we were. My mother's grandmother lived in Paducah, not far from Lubbock, with one of her sons. That's where Uncle Votie lived too. He was a rancher and, at one time, the Crosby County sheriff. Apparently he was an excellent marksman. The story got around that he could shoot a running rabbit with a pistol. I find that a little hard to believe, but it's part of Johnston family lore, so I feel compelled to pass it on.

It was kind of surprising to me how well my mother's family got along whenever they got together. My grandparents were so very strict that I hadn't seen much humor at home, but when we were with the uncles, we laughed and told family jokes and stories. It was always a fun time.

Life on the Farm

Though our family lacked emotional closeness, our lives were very much centered on home. Living on the farm meant there was always work to do. We grew a substantial garden, and I had to help with the weeding and picking. We grew beets; potatoes; and big, juicy tomatoes I bit into right off the vine.

In July, the sweet smell of ripe freestone peaches drew me to the orchard, where I would sit in the shade, leaning against the trunk, and eat my fill, juice dripping down my chin. We had a storm cellar with a metal-clad door that we piled into when a thunderstorm or tornado came through. At harvest time, I dried some of the peaches I picked, cutting them in half and laying them on this metal door. My efforts paid off in chewy, sweet dried fruit all winter long.

My mom and grandmother did a lot of canning. I still love beet pickles, but none are as good as my mom's. She added a little sugar. That might have had something to do with it.

Every year after the first cold front came through, we'd have hog killing. We waited for the freeze so the hog meat would keep better. Granddad was in his sixties at the time. He was fairly strong, but he needed a lot of help. Usually a neighbor would come, and we'd kill one or two hogs. They'd hit them with a sledgehammer to stun them, slit their throats, and hang them up on a rack to bleed out. After that, they'd slit the belly and pull out all the guts, then skin and butcher them.

I operated the sausage mill. As soon as they got into the butchering, they threw the less desirable parts on the table, and I dropped them in the mill and ground them. The women made the sausage containers out of flour sack sewed into a tube shape. We attached the tube to the mill, and as I turned the handle, the ground meat filled the sack. We tied the ends, rolled them in hog grease, and hung them in the smokehouse for a week or two. Somebody tended the fire all that time. We had no freezer or refrigerator, but the smoking cured the sausages and preserved them. We made enough sausages to feed us all year long.

My granddad grew oats for animal feed. Reapers pulled by

tractors cut the stalks, which would fall back on a belt that carried them to a trough. The reaper machine crushed the stalks together and bound them with twine that it tied and knotted. It was ingenious. The shocks fell into a holding bin and then onto the ground.

The machines worked in ever-narrowing circles toward the middle of the field, and the noise scared up all the baby rabbits that lived there. They'd keep running closer and closer to the center until they just had to escape. I loved watching them scatter in every direction. If we'd wanted to, we could have picked them off by the dozens and had a real feast, but we never shot them. We just let them go.

After the reaping and the rabbit run, a shocking crew came in and set the shocks upright, so when it rained, the water drained off quickly, and the grain kept for a week or two in the field without spoiling.

They didn't have combines in those days. When the time came for harvesting the grain, a crew with a big thresher powered by a belt-driven tractor came in. The crews threw the shocks onto a trailer or truck bed, which carried them to the thresher. They threw them into the bin, one or two shocks at a time, and the machine threshed out the chaff, which came out one end, and the grain, which came out the other. Nothing got wasted. The chaff got piled into a stack that we used to feed our animals.

I'm sure we were not well-off, but I never felt deprived. Life on the farm was simple and wholesome. It felt good to take part in growing and harvesting our food and caring for the animals. Too soon, that chapter of our family's life came to an end.

The Johnston Family Picks Up Stakes

In 1927, when I was heading into fourth grade, life took

another turn. Granddad had a heart attack, or so he said. My mother thought he was faking it. One night, he was up and groaning all night long. He kept everybody awake. In the morning, the doctor came out and told him his heart couldn't take all the heavy physical labor. Granddad didn't waste any time telling us the work was killing him, and we would have to give up the farm.

I hated to leave my horse and my dog but, of course, I didn't have any say about it. We moved ninety miles south to Sulphur, Oklahoma, named after the springs in the area. From our new house at the south end of town, Granddad walked about a mile to fetch the healing water every day. Bromide Hill rose about a thousand feet just behind the springs. He finally built up his strength to walk all the way to the top, and we tagged along. Granddad may or may not have had a heart attack, but the move to Sulphur definitely did him good.

The move did me a lot of good, too. My life changed dramatically soon after we got there. Every Sunday morning, my mother took my sister and me to a little Southern Baptist church right across the street from our house. I sat on those hard wood pews completely engrossed in the sermons. Though I was only ten years old, I understood the pastor's profound message. "Everybody is a sinner," he said, "but Jesus Christ died for our sins on the cross." I heard the Word of God loud and clear: All we have to do is accept these truths, believe, and have faith in His sufficiency to take care of the penalty for our sin. That's how I explained it to myself then, and that's how I see it still. I accepted Jesus Christ as my Savior right then and there.

* * *

Though my spiritual life began in that little church, at home I still had plenty of earthly responsibilities. We had a big garden in Sulphur, where we grew peas, beans, beets, tomatoes, and potatoes, and we had the two cows we brought down from Okemah. My mother and grandmother did the milking, but I had to feed the cows and muck out the stable now and then. That was terrible work. Inevitably, during milking time, the cow would poop and you'd just throw some hay on it and keep on going. Well, a week or ten days later, the hay would build up to the point where it had to be mucked out. That was my job. I had a pitchfork and I'd get in there and move it to the outside onto the compost heap. Later on we spread it on the gardens. Nothing got wasted in those days, and everybody had a job to do. In addition to keeping the stable clean, I cultivated the garden and picked the vegetables when they were ready.

In the summer, when I wasn't working, I was at the swimming pool. Sulphur, with its many cold springs, was a popular vacation spot. My mother bought me a season ticket to one of the four swimming pools for $5, and I lived in that cool water all summer long, except during chore time, of course.

During the school year I played stickball and softball with my friends. I always had a natural affinity for athletics and very little training. I just watched and learned. When I joined the high school football team, our coach didn't show us how to block or how to run patterns as a pass receiver. We just picked it up. Sulphur was a small town and we didn't have very many students, so even though I was not really that good at it, I played high school football for two years and lettered my senior year.

I never had any help with athletics, or mathematics, or anything else, for that matter. Throughout my life I've learned on my own and got to be pretty good at most things I tried. For instance, I don't remember how, but I taught myself to drive a car. My scoutmaster loaned me his, and off I went. I just liked to find out how things worked and how to use them. With no father and a granddad that was no help at all, I had to rely on myself.

A Passion Is Kindled

My abiding interest in airplanes began in Sulphur, and I know that my mother had more to do with that than naming me Orville. She grew up under the same dark cloud her father—my grandfather—cast over those closest to him. I imagine we shared a powerful desire to fly away from his house. Surely it was my mother who first took my hand and raced outside with me, pointing up at the sky. "Look, Orville. An airplane! The man is flying high up into the clouds." As I got older and began to think a lot about how things worked, I wanted to learn about the mystery of aeronautics and how man could build such a miraculous machine. All my childhood, whenever I heard the sound of an airplane engine overhead, I dropped whatever I was doing and ran out to see it.

The big news in May of 1927 was the first-ever transatlantic solo flight by Lindbergh. I was in the third grade, and that fall, after his heroic accomplishment, he flew his airplane, the Spirit of St. Louis, on a tour around the southern and central United States. He had promised to fly over every schoolhouse he could find, and one day, his course took him over ours in Sulphur. In the days leading up to his promised flight over our town, the newspaper was full of it. They estimated he would come over our school around ten o'clock in the morning, and he showed up right on time. He circled over us and dipped pretty low. We all waved to him and he leaned out the window and waved back. I'll never forget it. I can still see his face, half hidden behind his goggles, that leather helmet, his bright white shirt collar gleaming against his tanned skin, his tie flapping in the wind. I felt as if this gentleman adventurer's wave was an invitation. Through him, I saw far past my dour granddad's earthbound existence on the Oklahoma plains into a future worth aiming for.

Lindbergh's visit cemented my passion for flight, but I don't think I truly believed I would pilot an airplane one day until the following summer, when the barnstormer came to town. Barnstormers were veteran World War I pilots who bought surplus military airplanes after the war. There were lots of them, so these guys could buy them on the cheap and fly around the country, giving airplane rides for a fee. They went from one barnyard to another, and sometimes they stored the airplanes in the barn. One day, a barnstormer circled Sulphur. I was working in the garden when I heard him flying low, heading west of town. I dropped my hoe and jumped on my bicycle and rode out to where he landed.

"Yes, I'm going to give flying rides," he said. "Four dollars."

I bicycled back home, raced to my room, and cracked open my piggy bank. With four dollars in coin weighing down my pockets, I rode back out to the barnyard and got my very first airplane ride. We didn't go up for more than fifteen minutes. He just flew over the town—no aerobatics or anything fancy. Just a plane ride. But it was enough. That ride was worth every hard-earned penny, and it set me on an inevitable path. I just had to take a few detours before I got around to it.

* * *

My mother and sister and I never again had a house of our own. My granddad's house in Sulphur was my home until I left high school. Though Mom suffered emotionally when my dad left, she never had to suffer financially. Her parents gave us a roof over our heads, and her brothers, Bill and Ralph, helped us out financially. They were partners in the oil and gas business, and thanks to their support, we made it through the Depression with very little pain. When we moved off the farm in Okemah, the uncles bought it. They paid him a pretty good price for it. Far more than it was worth. So Granddad had a little money. As I recall, when we moved to Sulphur, Uncle Bill sent my mother a hundred dollars a month to live on. He was very kind to all of us.

FINDING MY WAY

School Days

After graduation from high school in Sulphur, I attended Kemper Military School & College in Booneville, Missouri. My Uncle Bill, who financed a good bit of my education beyond high school, thought I needed a more rounded outlook on life. He decided military school would be just the thing. It was kind of rigid, but I adapted to that very readily. I'd already learned quite a lot about authority from my granddad, but at Kemper I learned to respect it, and that helped me later on in the military.

In 1936, after one year at Kemper, I transferred to Oklahoma University in Norman.

Though I'd already completed a year of college, I still wasn't sure about a major. By nature or by choice, I'm very inquisitive. I've always wanted to know what was going on and what made things tick. I had built several model airplanes and fooled around with electric motors. That led me to believe I had mechanical skills, and that would be the way to go. I started out in petroleum engineering, thinking I might join my uncles in their oil and gas business. But after a year or two, I found I was having a little difficulty with some of the required studies. Crystallography baffled me. Normally I'm pretty good at picking things up, but trying to identify hundreds of crystals that all looked alike did me in. I switched over to mechanical, and to my great relief, did fairly well.

I didn't play any organized sports in college, though I played handball quite a bit and fooled around with sandlot baseball and softball. I wish I had gone out for the track team. It just never occurred to me. Considering my running success later in life, I have to think I would have been pretty good.

Once I left for college I never lived with my mother or grandparents again for any great length of time. I was always welcome back in Sulphur, but I worked every summer, usually in Okemah. Uncle Bill got me a job one year doing oilfield work. I was a roustabout—a general handyman. I wanted to get on a drilling rig and be a roughneck, but I didn't have enough experience. They paid me four dollars a day, which was a lot of money in 1935, and I saved enough to pay my tuition at OU the entire next year. The next summer, Uncle Bill got me a job in an abstract office in downtown Okemah.

I was grateful to Uncle Bill for paying my way through military school and helping me out at OU for the first couple of years. The last two years, though, I paid my own way, partly because he didn't think I was advancing quickly enough in life skills. He tried to get me a job with the newspaper in Okemah, and I turned it down. That may have given him the impression that I wasn't ambitious enough. I don't know. I have never been clear on what type of skills he thought I lacked, but by then I felt pretty confident I could take care of myself.

A Girl Named Esther Beth

As soon as I arrived at OU, I got involved in the Baptist Student Union. In a state school like OU, there isn't much emphasis on religion, and I really appreciated the Christian fellowship the Union provided. In my case, the BSU provided much more than that. In fact, you could say it changed my life. Serving on the executive council that first year, I met a fellow council member, a freshman named Esther Beth Shannon.

Nobody called her Esther. She never liked the name, so her close friends called her E.B. or Beth. I called her E.B. for many years, but later on I started calling her Beth. It just seemed to suit her.

Beth was dating somebody else, but I was a very patient man. I set my sights on her and never gave up. My approach was slow, but it was very effective. It took some time, but eventually I convinced her to come over to my side. For the next four years, she was a friend, a prayer mate, and a lover, in the good sense of the word.

It's unheard of these days, but I didn't kiss Beth until I had known her about three years. I was afraid I'd upset her. I didn't want to endanger my relationship by going too fast. Nevertheless, by the time she was a junior and I was a senior, our future together was pretty well determined. I never did ask her to marry me. We just took it for granted.

Like my mom, Beth's mother faced challenges in raising her children on her own. Beth had a sister, Ruth, who was three years older. Their father died of a heart attack when Beth was a sophomore in high school. Her mother didn't have as many years to worry about keeping a roof over their heads, but she had to work much harder to keep the family going than my mother did.

Beth's father was a geologist with the Oklahoma Geological Survey until he lost his job during the Depression. The governor of Oklahoma at the time was named Alfalfa Bill Murray.

That's what they called him. Determined to keep expenses down, he cancelled all the appropriations to the Oklahoma Geological Survey. That put Beth's dad out of a job.

He tried to make a go of it financially by doing contract geological work for oil and gas companies, but there wasn't very much work in the early days of the Depression, and he gradually fell into debt. The stress and disappointment might have brought on the heart attack. I don't know. But a couple of days after he died, the family held a memorial service for him, and that same day the creditors came to take the furniture he had hocked out of the house. He had mortgaged the furniture just to put bread on the table.

His brother came down from Indiana to help out, and he managed to stave off the creditors. He told them, "Come back tomorrow or the next day." In the meantime, he rented a furnished apartment for the grieving family and gave them a little money to help them get started.

Thanks to her husband's association with the Geological Survey, Beth's mom got a job as a secretary to a geology professor at Oklahoma University. She held that job seven or eight years, until she was seventy years old. She would have stayed on, but her eyesight began to fail.

Beth and her sister supplemented their mother's income with twenty-five-cent-an-hour babysitting jobs. That's how they helped pay their way through Oklahoma University, which, at that time, cost $50 a year for in-state tuition. Working together, they were able to make it through some pretty tough years.

Our similar backgrounds cemented our relationship. We both came from families who managed to keep bread on the table because everybody pitched in. Neither of us expected life to be easy, and that prepared us for the bumps along the way.

Beth and I believed that God's will for people is one woman, one man for life and no sexual experience until marriage. That has sort of fallen by the wayside, but it worked for us, and I think it worked for our kids. Right from the beginning, we were about as close as two people can be, and I attribute our deep intimacy to our devotion to God and our willingness to always make things work. We talked about everything, we compromised, and we supported each other. Even during the tough times, our love never wavered.

Into the Sky

My ambition to be a pilot got a boost during my senior year at OU. The government announced that it would start a flying training program for eligible college students. I think they sensed the inevitability of US involvement in WWII and the coming need for many pilots. OU offered the training, and I qualified. In early January 1940, I entered the ground school program. Flight training began shortly thereafter. A flying school in Oklahoma City relocated a few Piper Cubs and instructors to a field near OU in Norman. It was only a grass strip, but it was good enough.

I did well enough to solo after the minimum eight hours dual flight time, and I will never forget the exhilaration of that first flight on my own. It was almost as if I was having an out-of-body experience. I was on my own and could go anywhere or do anything I wanted to. I had dreamed of that kind of freedom since seeing Lindbergh wave at us from the Spirit of St. Louis. And, twelve years later, I possessed a bit of that sense of freedom and adventure he inspired in me.

Meanwhile, I was nearing the end of the five-year mechanical engineering degree program. As I got closer to graduating, I had to start thinking about a career. I considered going to work for my uncles, who were partners in Johnston & Johnston, their successful oil and gas company. Uncle Bill had helped two of my cousins into the business, and I had reason to believe he would have gotten me a job.

Though I could have had a very lucrative career, I decided against the oil business. I imagined following my passion for flying instead. Considering how much money I could have made with my uncles, that probably seemed like a pretty bad idea. Still, following your passion is an acceptable alternative. My family assumed I would enter pilot training after graduation. And then I abandoned that dream.

A New Path

Complicated emotions led me to decide against a career in aviation. As a young Christian, like many others, I began to have some doubts along the way. Had I truly committed my life to God? Did God believe my decision to accept Christ as my Lord and Savior? I was part of a very mature group of Christian young people in college, and through our many discussions, I had come to understand that true commitment to God is not only about having faith in the Lord Jesus Christ. That word *Lord* means "master." It means Jesus Christ is your Master, and you serve Him. I understood this intellectually, but I wasn't convinced I had reached that point in my heart.

The self-doubt in my willingness to serve the Lord drove my decision to commit my life's work to Him. I wanted to prove to God that I had really chosen to follow Jesus at the tender age of ten. Or maybe I wanted to prove it to myself. Giving up a career in oil and gas was not that hard, but choosing religious work over flying airplanes was very difficult indeed. Looking back on it now, I wanted God to know I really meant business.

I count it as one of the decisions that changed my life forever.

A LIFE OF SERVICE BEGINS

The Seminary

Though I was convinced I ought to be in some kind of work for God, I didn't know what I should do. Lacking the necessary communication skills, I didn't think I'd make a good preacher. I thought I might be able to do something in music, which I loved, and with two high school courses in music theory, I knew I had the aptitude. I played the mellophone (like a French horn) in the high school marching band and violin in the orchestra. At OU, I played the French horn and sang in the Glee Club. Of course, I had always sung in church choirs, and my mom had even paid for my singing lessons. I decided music would be the way to go.

One of the best training grounds for church work is still the Southwestern Baptist Theological Seminary in Fort Worth,

Texas, the largest seminary in the world. In 1940, after graduation from OU with a degree in engineering, I turned my back on everyone's expectations of me and moved to Texas to attend the seminary.

Beth would have been there with me if she hadn't developed Malta fever, a disease that results from ingesting unpasteurized milk. The two-month hospitalization cost her a semester, and she stayed behind at OU. That didn't make any difference in our relationship. We had already sealed it. We were engaged by the time I graduated from college, and, after finishing up at OU, she joined me in Fort Worth.

God Sets Me Straight

My seminary experience should have closed the door on any prospects of flying airplanes, but God has always been in charge of my life, and this was no exception. I enrolled at the Seminary on September 10, 1940. On October 29, federal officials in Washington, D.C., ceremoniously picked the first round of draftees. We had been assigned our selective service numbers when we registered for the draft a year or two earlier. In Washington, D.C., they set up a giant fishbowl and filled it with capsules, each one containing a number from 1 to 7,836. The secretary of war, Henry Stimson, picked out the first one. It contained the number 158. That meant all the young men in the US with a draft number ending in 158 could expect a phone call. After a photo op with Stimson and President Roosevelt, flunkies took over the random fishing for capsules. Thinking they wouldn't need very many men, they only picked out five hundred numbers that day. So help me, the eighth number drawn was mine. I knew I was on my way.

I heard from the draft board the very next week. "I don't want to be in the walking army," I said. "Can I be in the Air Corps as a flying cadet?"

I had taken the secondary flight course while I was living in Fort Worth, and that's when I fell truly and deeply in love with flying. I was training in a beautiful low-wing, the Ryan ST-A, with aerobatic capability. Once my instructor showed me how to do aerobatics, I spent most of my solo time practicing. He taught me a very valuable lesson that carried over into life on the ground: "Be very attentive to the variations in airspeed or altitude or other parameters that the instructor points out. With his experience, he sees what you have yet to learn to notice."

Though the military had no knowledge of my flight training, I was approved for the Air Corps and sent to Fort Sill, Oklahoma, for a physical. After passing, I reported back to the draft board. "We'll keep you posted," they said.

They didn't exactly stay in close touch. I finished out the school year at the seminary and returned to Sulphur. All summer long, I waited, thinking I'd hear from them any day. In September, they finally wrote me: "You're in a class of Army Air Forces cadets starting November first in San Diego, California." On June 20, 1941, the Army Air Corps had effectively been abolished and replaced with the newly established Army Air Forces (AAF). I didn't care what they called it. I was just glad to be assigned to the air, not the ground.

Years later, when I tried to come to terms with what happened, I could only draw one conclusion: The draft call was God's way of turning me around. I had turned my back on flying to prove to God that I had fully committed my life to Him. But God knows everything. My decision proved my commitment to God to *myself*. God already knew that I would devote my life to His service, and He gave flying back to me in a very dramatic way. As it turned out, my talents as a pilot served Him far better than anything I could have done as a church worker.

God always has something better for me than I think I

deserve. The circumstances of my early life—abandoned by my dad, reared by a single mother with limited means, and by grandparents who withheld affection from each other and from us—did not bode well for a glowing future. And yet, God has seen fit time and time again to bless me with experiences and relationships that have enriched my life beyond measure.

FLIGHT TRAINING ON A WING AND A PRAYER

The Sunday the World Changed

As US involvement in the war began to appear likely, the military took over the flight school of Ryan Aeronautical, an airplane manufacturing company in San Diego. Ryan had built the Spirit of Saint Louis, which Lindbergh had flown across the Atlantic and over my school in Sulphur, Oklahoma.

The AAF told us to expect about nine months of flight training—three months in primary, three months in basic, and three months in advanced. Ryan provided civilian instructors for our primary training—both ground school and flying. After that initial phase, we were sent to an army base for basic and advanced. As instructed, I reported for duty in

San Diego on November 1, 1941.

On a Sunday five weeks later, I left the base to attend church, as usual. Following the service, a nice couple invited me to go home for lunch with them. Afterward, I played with their two young children, and at two or three o'clock, their dad turned on the radio to listen to the afternoon music programs.

We were enjoying *Sammy Kaye's Sunday Serenade* when a newscaster interrupted with a special news bulletin.

"The Japanese have attacked Pearl Harbor, Hawaii, by air, President Roosevelt has just announced. The attack also was made on all air and naval activities on the principal island of Oahu," he said.

A correspondent in Washington, D.C., reiterated the news and concluded, "A Japanese attack on Pearl Harbor would naturally mean war."

I returned to my base immediately and checked in. Back then, we didn't have CNN and instant updates. In those first days, it was hard to get a handle on what was happening and what to expect. News filtered in gradually, but the effect of the raids was immediate. Anger, grief, and fear charged the atmosphere. Our lives changed in an instant and forever.

Rampant fear that the Japanese would attack the West Coast with aircraft carriers or submarines pervaded the national consciousness. We were on high alert. The West Coast blacked out all the windows in the factories in case of attack. All the airplane factories ramped up production, operating night and day.

As the build-up to war picked up steam, the training course sped up considerably. Instead of three months each in primary, basic, and advanced, they shortened the time to two months. After six months and twenty-two days of flight training, I earned my wings and became a commissioned officer, a second lieutenant in the Army Air Forces.

Instructor Training with Jimmy Stewart

Following primary training in San Diego, I went to Lemoore Basic Flying School in central California, a newly built military training field. I flew the BT-13, which wasn't as nimble as the PT-22 I flew in San Diego, but a very reliable trainer. My instructor enjoyed "buzzing" ("flat hatting" in Navy lingo), which is flying very low, a highly entertaining experience with the ground rushing by underneath you and trees flashing past at eye level. Though it's dangerous and frowned upon in civilian life, it is sometimes a necessary maneuver in combat, and it came in handy several times when I was ferrying airplanes for JAARS.

The accelerated training schedule gave me only two months at Lemoore before being transferred to Stockton, California, for the advanced twin-engine training course. This was an exhilarating time, but it was also a difficult time for Beth and me. We were engaged, but we couldn't get married. I couldn't support a wife until I graduated from flight training and started drawing a decent salary. Meanwhile, after attending the seminary on a scholarship, Beth thought she ought to repay that in some manner, so she took a job as a secretary for three church colleges in Springfield, Missouri. She committed to one year, and we planned to get married on June 1, 1943.

My instructor in advanced training school told me he would recommend I become an instructor. I asked him not to. I was a crazy, mixed-up kid. I wanted to get married, but that wasn't going to happen for a year, which felt like forever. Maybe I just wanted to be sent overseas to put my mind on something else. I don't know. For whatever reason, I asked him not to recommend me. Lucky for me, he did it anyway. Looking back on it, I am grateful. He probably saved my life.

Following graduation from Advanced Training School, the Air Force sent me to Sacramento, California, for one month of instructor training at Mather Air Force Base. The military considered one month of training to fly twin-engine airplanes to be enough, and it was.

I had very rigorous flying instruction in an airplane they call the AT-9, a twin-engine advanced trainer aircraft. It's a hot airplane, not slow by any means, and it was a good trainer for the advanced bombers they were bringing out. The AT-9 was as fast as any of the single-engine trainers we had. It was a really nice airplane. I loved it, and I ate that training up.

I shared my time at Mather with Jimmy Stewart. He and I were in the same squadron. He instructed at Mather for two or three months, and though he was not my instructor, I flew formation with him several times. He was a very nice guy, very friendly. I wish I'd gotten him to sign my logbook. I don't know why I didn't. He certainly would have obliged. Several years later, he was in a film called *Strategic Air Command* that featured, among other airplanes, the B-36, which I flew during the Korean Conflict. They filmed a lot of scenes at Carswell in Fort Worth, my B-36 base.

A Diamond for My Girl

Once I graduated as a second lieutenant in May 1942, I started drawing a salary of about $200 a month plus an additional $100 in flight pay. With that money burning a hole in my pocket, I went to the Granat Jewelry Company in San Francisco and bought an engagement ring—a meridian diamond set in platinum. Gold would have been fine, but I wanted the best. It cost $500 or $600, and I didn't have enough money to pay for it. They let me put 10 percent down, and I agreed to send them a check once a month until it was paid for.

Thinking back, I can't imagine they would sell a young soldier a ring on credit. I could have been shipped out any time, and who knows if I would have made it back. I consider that a great kindness, the sort of thing that people did in those days. It certainly wouldn't happen today.

Beth was living in Norman with her sister and mother at the time, and I sent the ring to her. She held off opening the package until we could talk on the telephone. That took another few days, but finally we set the wedding date, and I wrote to the jeweler and ordered the wedding band.

FIRST ASSIGNMENT: ROSWELL, NEW MEXICO

After completing instructor flying school at Mather, I was qualified to serve as a full-fledged instructor. My first assignment was a base in Roswell, New Mexico. Just a few years after my tenure there, Roswell gained notoriety for an alleged UFO crash landing nearby. But while I was there, it was nothing more than an out-of-the-way town on the dry plains of the Southwest—a perfect place to teach young men how to fly airplanes.

I enjoyed teaching, and I learned more about flying than I ever would have if I had gone overseas. However, the demands of the war turned the job into a test of endurance for instructors and students alike. After Pearl Harbor, we were so short of pilots that we were rushing them through training. An astonishing number of instructors and cadets were killed in the training command during World War II. I found this on the World War II Foundation website: According to the *Army Air Force Statistical Digest,* in less than four years (December 1941–August 1945), the US Army Air Force lost 14,903 pilots, aircrew, and assorted personnel inside the continental US. The losses were the result of 52,651 aircraft accidents (6,039 involving fatalities) in forty-five months.[1] I count myself lucky to have escaped harm. I lost a good friend in one accident, and one of my students was killed.

They cranked up the output of the airplane factories too, turning out B-17s, B-24s, training planes, light bombers, and Navy planes at an enormous rate. Ford had built a large automobile assembly plant at the Willow Run manufacturing complex in Michigan, and this was converted to an airplane factory, where they turned out one B-24 every fifty-five minutes.

We worked overtime and then some to prepare the pilots to fly those planes in combat. Most of our service pilots received a lot more training than Germans did, particularly at the end of the war. I heard that Germans were so short of pilots that they were just checking them out with very few hours and then putting them in an airplane . . . if they had one.

The last phase of training for the flying cadets was advanced flying training school. They graduated as second lieutenants with their pilot's wings, and afterwards were assigned to a base to train for a month or so in the airplane they would be flying. By then they had about two hundred hours, which

---

1. "WWII Air Force Facts." WWII Foundation.
http://www.wwiifoundation.org/students/wwii-aircraft-facts/.

is not very much. Considering the circumstances, they were accomplished pilots.

After their flight training, the newly commissioned second lieutenants went off to fighter school or a bomb squadron training base to prepare for actual combat. They were there a month or more, and that added another hundred hours or so to their flying experience. Our pilots went into combat with a minimum of three hundred hours. It was as grueling for the instructors as it was for the cadets, and though I couldn't imagine it getting worse, it did.

Training under the Gun

In January 1943, our entire squadron was transferred to La Junta, Colorado. The demand for pilots pressed in on us. Training became our entire focus in life. Eating and sleeping took a back seat. For two consecutive months, we went to the airport after breakfast and flew until lunchtime. Normally we would have briefed the students that afternoon on the lessons they had learned, but we conducted a very hurried briefing while we ate. At one, we returned to the airport to fly another group of students until five and brief them before dinner. It was a rigorous work day that meant getting up at six, eating breakfast at seven, working eight hours, and eating a hurried dinner at six or seven before dropping into a short sleep.

The next month, we got a little behind due to bad weather, and the command doubled up the training. I still can't believe we did this, but it actually happened. We flew double duty from midnight until noon. It's almost impossible to understand how difficult that was. It wreaked havoc with our circadian rhythms, which affected our sleep/wake cycles and, in turn, our ability to think and react. I'd rather fly all night long than go to work at midnight and fly until noon.

We'd report around eleven at night, brief the students, and

fly from midnight until four or five. After a hurried briefing, we'd go back to the mess hall and eat breakfast. At 6:30 or 7:00 a.m., we'd get another group of students and fly with them until noon. Then we'd brief them before we could go and get some sleep. We reported each night at 11 p.m. and got off at 1 p.m. the next day. Another set of trainers took over when we were sleeping, so the training was going on around the clock.

* * * One of our major aims was to teach pilots to fly in close formation with other planes, night or day. You have to remember, in night flying, if you don't have stars and a moon, you're dependent on your instruments to tell you what you're doing. It's very difficult and imperative that you watch the instruments all the time. That's why I hated formation flying at night. I loved it in the daytime. You could see the sky and the ground out of the corner of your eye. At night, it was instruments only, and there were no visual reference points on the ground. In Colorado after eight or nine o'clock at night, everyone who lived on a farm turned their lights out and went to bed. It was just black as the ace of spades.

One of the accidents at Roswell involved the nighttime flight of a team leader who took off and flew a big arc. His students took off behind him and cut across the corner to join him. Though it was dark, they weren't using instruments. They concentrated on the visual reference to the lead plane. For some reason, the team leader failed to gain altitude. The students followed him, and all three planes flew into the ground. Thankfully, it was level ground, so the impact was akin to landing wheels up. They just skidded to a stop. Nobody was hurt, and the airplanes weren't even terribly damaged.

Other accidents ended in tragedy. One dark, moonless night we got the word that a plane had crashed in the traffic pattern. We jumped in our cars and headed to the south end of the field. The traffic pattern had widened out and the planes were four or five miles south of the airport. One of the planes got out of the traffic pattern and lost his reference to sky and earth and just flew into the ground. That crash killed both pilots. There were lots of accidents like that. I don't want to dwell on it, but it wasn't without its hazards. It was a rushed-up deal. They needed pilots so very badly, so we did what we had to do.

We had three or four instances of a plane going down and disappearing. We lost one on a cross-country run somewhere between Roswell and Phoenix. The search party consisted of twenty or thirty airplanes, which was well worth the effort considering we might find the pilot alive. Each group of five or ten had a designated area to search. We flew in parallel lines, three or four airplanes stacked up, looking for any sign of the downed airplane. Sadly, our efforts didn't pay off for that one or many of the others.

On the plus side, we were flying B-25s, exactly the type of plane I had always wanted to fly. It's a medium-size twin-engine bomber, but it's the one that Col. Jimmy Doolittle used to raid Japan. I couldn't have been more surprised. Up until then, all we'd flown were little bitty twin-engine and single-engine airplanes. Then, around November of 1942, we got the B- 25s, and that made me happy.

That Doolittle raid was in May of 1942. I was halfway through flying school at the time. We just heard hazy reports that we had bombed Tokyo. Later it came out that they were B-25s taking off from an aircraft carrier. The B-25 was a beautiful airplane. I thought it was just wonderful that I got to fly one.

The Chinese Students

The US government had established a policy of recruiting young Chinese Nationalist men to undergo flight training on the B-25s in the US. They would then return and serve in the military effort against the Axis in the Far East. Almost all my

American students were cadets who, upon graduation, were commissioned second lieutenants. The Chinese students, on the other hand, had all gotten their commissions, so they were already second lieutenants or the equivalent. I had Chinese students twice at La Junta, where they came for the final two-month phase of their flight training.

Some of them had never driven a car, and here they were flying a B-25 bomber. A commandant of their group acted as an interpreter on the ground, but in the air we had to make do with a lot of hand signs. They were fairly proficient in English, but not completely so. Nevertheless, we managed. They all graduated and got their wings, except for one who was killed in an accident.

One night the Chinese students were doing team rides. In the initial phase of their instruction, the instructor would ride in the right seat, a student in the left seat, and another student observed from behind. The students would trade off shooting landings or other maneuvers. That way each of them could see what the other did and the mistakes they made, and they would profit from their fellow students' experiences. It worked well, and after the instructor had flown with the students long enough to consider them capable, they would go up on team rides on their own.

We had a grueling schedule for the Chinese, often flying from midnight until four or five in the morning. Your brain just doesn't work right under those conditions. Night landings were more difficult because it's just a different sensation to approach a partially lit runway. The Chinese adapted pretty well, but on one occasion we were shooting landings and doing follow-through takeoffs. That is, we would take off and climb to traffic-pattern altitude. Then we'd circle around and come back in and land. Instead of stopping and taxiing back to the takeoff position, we'd slow down enough to call it a successful landing. There would be just enough runway left to accommodate another takeoff. That gave us more landing practice in any given period.

Sometimes we did the full landing, coming to a full stop, just to be sure the students knew how to do it. The night of the accident, we were doing full-stop landings, and two Chinese students were on a team ride without the instructor. The student pilots took turns in the left and right seats. After landing, they taxied back to the takeoff run-up area. With the propeller-driven airplanes, you had to stop before you taxied onto the runway and check the magneto, mixture control, and propeller control. You would do that on an area offsetting the runway itself to avoid disrupting the other pilots landing and taking off. After those checks, if the tower gave you permission, you would taxi onto the runway and take off.

The two Chinese students had made a takeoff and a landing and had taxied back and parked in the run-up area. The B-25 did not have a steerable nose wheel. You had to use rudders and brakes and power to change your direction. Sometimes the nose wheel would swivel around to a point where, if you allowed it to, it would be hard to get centered again. We were cautioned not to let it get that far unless we were forced to in order to make a very tight turn. Once you got the nose wheel over there, it was hard to get it back in the centered position.

The Chinese students made the mistake of turning around into the wind, and they stopped the airplane with the nose wheel all the way to the right. It's very difficult to get it straightened out when you're stopped. You have to use a whole lot of power on the good engine on that side. They had been cautioned about it, but apparently they didn't understand. They decided that one of them would go down and try to straighten it out by hand. That's impossible. Hercules couldn't have done it. The propeller arc passes within about three feet of that nose wheel on both sides, and the doomed Chinese pilot walked right into the propeller. He never saw it. It hit him in the head and killed him instantly.

We experienced that kind of tragedy time after time in the training command. Not to the extent that they did in combat, but we lost a lot of crews that way. I think we realized, subconsciously perhaps, that you had to maintain a sense of proportion about grief. If you let it take control of your life, you lost it. You had to keep on with the mission even though you were losing people. We did not nearly approach the hazards of combat flying, but we did lose a few, quite a few, and they were considered the necessary side effects of intense training. It's no surprise that the accident rate was so high. I feel very fortunate to have lived through it.

Up, Up, and Away

As a flying officer, if I flew three and a half hours a month, I drew hazard pay, which was another 50 percent more than my base pay. Naturally, we all thought it imperative we get in our flying time every month to draw that extra dollar. I think I was making about $250 a month base pay at the time of my separation, which meant I got an extra $125 if I flew three and a half hours.

After flying thirty hours or more during the week, the other pilots and I had neither the time nor the desire to spend another minute in the cockpit. But on the weekends, when we had a day off, we did personal proficiency flying. That is, we checked out an airplane and did anything we wanted to—aerobatics, formation work with another airplane, or flying for the sheer pleasure of enjoying God's earth.

I checked an airplane out on Friday afternoon a couple times and went to Springfield, Missouri, where Beth was living before we got married. I flew to Oklahoma City and spent the night there, then flew on to Springfield the next day. I got there before noon, and we had a few hours together until late afternoon. Then I had to fly back home. That was a lot of flying for a short visit, but it was well worth it.

The other instructors and I often practiced dogfighting. Another pilot and I would check out T-6 single-engine trainers, a very maneuverable plane with good power for its weight. We'd go out and dogfight for thirty minutes to an hour, just trying to get each other's tails, firing guns at each other—simulated, of course. The simulated combat got my adrenaline pumping, and if I had ever gone to combat in a fighter plane, the practice would have been very helpful, but I never went to combat in any kind of an airplane, much less a fighter.

During our dogfighting practice drills, we started out together and flew alongside each other. Then we broke off, dove, and came back as if we were enemy fighters. After we passed each other, we tried to get on the tail of the other airplane to shoot him down. The only guns on a fighter airplane were on the front, pointing forward. There was no shooting backwards or sideways.

The idea was to pass your opponent without getting shot, then swing around and maneuver your plane to end up on the other guy's tail. It was a matter of skill. If you spotted another airplane, you'd approach him from the rear and dive on him. That was the ideal, but in real combat, there might be times when you would see a fighter approaching, and you wouldn't want to turn around because then he'd be on your tail. Basically, you're firing and he's firing, and the first one to hit wins. I'm just glad my only dogfighting experience was with blanks.

Towing the Line, Most of the Time

The military way of doing things often made little sense. We just shook our heads and followed orders. After the war, when I was stationed in Big Spring, Texas, I got orders to travel by rail to Denver, Colorado, and ferry an airplane. That wasn't unusual, but the story gets weirder. There were two Air Force bases in Denver, and they had pilots at both fields. I was to report to one of them, and my orders were to ferry an airplane from one field to the other field ten miles away. They sent me up from Big Spring, Texas, to do a job anyone stationed in Denver could have done. Maybe there was a reason. Who knows? The military does things that ensure survival. Plus, nobody wants to take the blame if something goes wrong. I imagine my trip had less to do with survival and more to do with somebody covering his rear end.

Most of the time that I served in the Air Force, I bowed to the military way. But near the end of the war, an opportunity arose—a calculated risk I simply could not refuse. In late 1944 or early 1945, the military decided to turn La Junta into a B-17 base, and they dispersed all the B-25s to other bases around the country. I was a squadron commander with three or four instructors under me, and each of them had four or five students. To deliver the planes, flight leaders would lead three planes to the delivery base and leave two there. Then the crews would pile into the lead airplane and fly back to La Junta.

Our squadron was charged with delivering two of the B-25s to Nellis Air Force Base near Las Vegas, Nevada. On one of our flights, I decided to have some fun. I was leading the two other airplanes, flying across the flat, dry Colorado Plateau in the area of the Four Corners and the Navajo reservation. Knowing exactly where we were headed, I couldn't resist making a slight change in our course.

We were flying at 180 to 200 mph, in deep and cloudless blue, across barren gray and yellow ground far below. In the distance, a thin line at the horizon glowed pink against the midday sky. In a matter of moments, that hint of pink burst into a vast expanse of God's creation, and I dropped that B-25 down into the Grand Canyon.

Our three airplanes flew just below the rim from the eastern edge of the canyon following the path of the Colorado River, a ribbon of green carving through the sedimentary layers of limestone, sandstone, and shale. We probably had a couple of hundred feet of clearance on each side. More at some points. Less at others. It felt much narrower, as if our wings would touch the red, pink, and coral sedimentary layers of the mightiest canyon of them all. We flew below the rim all the way, dipping even further down as we approached Lake Mead at the western edge of the canyon.

What a feeling that was. A sense of freedom and release replaced the weariness and strain we had lived with for so long. Most certainly God pointed the way that day, wanting me to see the wonder of this world He made for us. All these years later, the memory of it still gives me a thrill.

A Long Wait for a Hurried Wedding

Thanks to my Chinese students, Beth and I did not have the hometown wedding we had envisioned. The training sessions lasted two months, and normally we had a week off in between. We planned to celebrate our wedding during that break on June 1, 1943, in Norman, Oklahoma. I had five copies of my military orders in my hand, granting me leave for June 1 to 5. On May 31, the orders were cancelled. The military had decided to give the graduating Chinese students gunnery training, and my attendance was required.

Here's another example of the military way: They had yet to create the gunnery instruction program for the Chinese. That's how the military does things to this day. It's so cumbersome. It's so difficult to get things done right. We eventually gave them a little gunnery training, but it was a month later. There was no reason they couldn't have let me go on my leave. All my friends, including my best man, had been instructing American students. They all got their leaves, and they all went home.

I sat around for a month waiting for the gunnery training to begin. As soon as it was over, the Chinese returned to the Pacific and joined the fight. I wish I had been able to keep track of them. I heard one of my students sank a Japanese cruiser. That's highly speculative, but I like to think it's true.

Beth and I could easily have gotten married on June 1 as planned, and returned to the base before instruction commenced, but I didn't know that at the time. When they cancelled my leave, I called Beth and said, "Do you want to wait another two months or come to La Junta and get married?"

To my great relief and happiness, she said, "I'll be on the next train."

Beth; her sister, Ruth; her mother, Mary; and my mother traveled from Norman to La Junta by train. Ruth's husband, a doctor, was stationed in Papua New Guinea at the time. The four women left Norman about five in the afternoon and arrived in Manhattan, Kansas, around midnight.

Manhattan was a switching depot for the Santa Fe Chief coming down from Chicago. They caught the Chief for the final stretch into La Junta a couple hours later. The train was packed with servicemen, and none of them would surrender their seats, so the women sat on their luggage for the five-hour ride.

I met them at the train station at seven o'clock in the morning and took Beth straight to the base hospital for the blood tests. It was nip and tuck getting everything done, but it worked out.

We got married June 3, 1943, at seven o'clock in the evening in the base chapel with a military chaplain officiating. Since many of the instructors were gone on leave, there were more Chinese than Americans in attendance. Malcolm Ritchie, a classmate of mine all through training, was to have been my best man. He and I were close friends until he died a few years ago. Unfortunately, he couldn't be there for the biggest day of my life. I had to scrounge around and get another best man. He wasn't my best friend by any means, but he stood up for me, and Beth and I got married, and it took.

Thanks to the military's disorganization, Beth and I enjoyed a twenty-eight day honeymoon. They had to design and set up the gunnery training course for the Chinese students, and it took a month to do that. All I did for four weeks was sign in at eight o'clock in the morning and come back home and enjoy the rest of the day with my bride. Those were wonderful days for Beth and me.

* * *

Our first home was the La Junta Motor Court. There were not many travelers staying at tourist courts in those days, so they were taking people on a daily, weekly, or monthly basis. Eastern Colorado does not have much to offer. The land, flat as a platter, is irrigated by the Arkansas River, and very profitably so. We once drove up to the headwaters of the Arkansas, near Leadville. It's a beautiful mountain stream up there and gathers momentum as it flows down through Colorado. When it gets to Pueblo and east into the plains of Colorado, most of the water has been taken out for irrigation. By the time the Arkansas gets to La Junta, it's just a sand flat with a little trickle running through it. It's kind of tragic that such a beautiful river comes to nothing so fast.

We spent our first weeks together in that bleak little town, but on my next leave, we had a real honeymoon. We spent a week in Colorado Springs at the original Antlers Hotel and visited all the sights—the Garden of the Gods, the Royal Gorge, and Pike's Peak. We meant to climb to the top of Pike's Peak but ran into a snowstorm that forced us back down. We probably wouldn't have made it to the top anyway. At ten thousand feet or so, where we turned back, it was snowy and cold. Forty years later, we climbed a much higher mountain together, but that story comes later.

My First and Last Passenger

Beth and I didn't make it to the top of Pike's Peak, but we had plenty of other adventures in our years together, and a lot of them were much higher than ten thousand feet. I started flying at age twenty-two, when I was still at OU. Beth was my first passenger. She liked to say she would fly with me anywhere, anytime, and she did. Fifty-seven years later, she was my last passenger.

A few days after I got my private license I rented a Piper Cub and took Beth up for her second airplane ride. She had ridden with a barnstormer a year or two before. The Piper Cub was an easy airplane to fly, though test pilot Max Stanley saw it a bit differently. "The Piper Cub is the safest airplane to fly," he said. "It can just barely kill you."

Beth's first ride with me could have been her last if she had been a lot less adventuresome. The Piper is a tandem, so she sat behind me. For the most part, she enjoyed it, but when I was circling her house, she started losing interest. She had told her mother to look out for us. Sure enough, I saw her out in the backyard waving a bed sheet. I don't know that Beth saw anything at all. She might have had her eyes closed, too worried about falling out of the sky.

You see, the only way you can turn an airplane is to bank it. You can't skid it around like a car. It just won't turn. You put one wing down, and that keeps you turning in place. Beth got a little worn out with the process. She didn't even like the turning, much less the banking. Nevertheless, the next time I asked her to go flying with me, she agreed. I just had to promise not to do any fancy stuff.

By the time Beth joined me in La Junta, she felt much more comfortable in the air, and she flew with me quite often. The military's personal proficiency flying program was extremely liberal. We could take our wives up for a flight once every six months. I took Beth up four times in everything from a single-engine trainer plane to a twin-engine AT-17 to a B-25— the military combat bomber. I'm still astounded when I think about it. I took my wife up for a thirty-minute ride in a B-25!

Beth was a seasoned flier when I began ferrying small aircraft to distant missions, and she accompanied me on several of those flights. For our last ferry flight together, we flew halfway around the world across the Pacific Ocean. The trip was a testament to the strength and endurance of our bond. For seventy-two hours we were crammed into the cockpit of a small twin-engine airplane, and we shared that tiny space with several hundred gallons of avgas. It was uncomfortable, and worse, it was dangerous. But we enjoyed every moment of that last flight together.

Bakersfield and Our First Baby

Once we completed the transfers of all the B-25s to Nevada, we were sent to an Air Force tactical unit in the San Joaquin Valley of California. Our first child, Orville Curtis Rogers, Jr., was born there June 12, 1945, in a Bakersfield hospital.

Back then, it was normal to keep mother and baby in the hospital for a week, and Beth and Curtis were no exception. Nowadays they've gotten smart. They realize that giving birth is a normal part of life. Primitive women gave birth squatting in a field and went back to work right after. Not that I'm recommending that, but Beth's long stay in the hospital wore her out more than it strengthened her.

Fortunately, my duties at the base were very light in those days. I was between jobs, in a holding pattern. I just checked in and checked out, which gave me a lot of free time to really pitch in with the housework and the baby.

While Beth was recovering, I drove her and baby Curtis up to the Sierras to see Yosemite and Kings Canyon National Parks. We spent the night in the valley and then drove into Yosemite and spent a full day up there. I was driving a two-door 1938 powder blue Plymouth. It had about thirty thousand miles on it when I bought it upon graduation from flying school. That was our transportation for several years. For some reason, I got the idea to put a spotlight on it. You don't see them anymore, but they were kind of the vogue in those days, and they came in handy every now and then.

I installed the spotlight myself. It sat on the outside of the car, by the driver's window. You could control it from the inside, make it go up and down and sideways. I had enough experience with electricity to know it should not be on the same circuit with the other lights. If I had installed it incorrectly, it could have interfered with the electrical system and blown out the headlights. Wearing my mechanical engineering hat, I put in a separate fuse that connected directly to the battery, making the spotlight operate independently from the other lights.

Coming down out of Yosemite in the dark after watching the sunset, we had barely gotten out of the park when every light in the car went off. But the spotlight worked! I consider that one of my greatest engineering achievements.

The Japanese Surrender

Curtis was three weeks old when I received my orders to go to B-17 training in Lovington, New Mexico. This was a bittersweet assignment. I wanted to fly the big airplanes, and in Bakersfield I was about to have the opportunity again. But being married and the father of my first child, I thought the B-17 training would be the responsible thing to do. I thought

I would be a more qualified applicant for an airline job if I had some four-engine time.

Traveling by car from Bakersfield to Lovington, we went from the frying pan into the fire. I bought a swamp cooler for the Plymouth, an aluminum tube that attached to the passenger window. It had water in the bottom and cylinders that rotated when the car was in motion. The core had wood shavings soaked in the water, and when the breeze blew over them, it cooled the inside of the car. It worked real well for about a hundred-mile stretch. Out there in the dry heat, you'd have to replenish the water that often. So that's how we crossed the Great American Desert in the Plymouth in the middle of the summer of 1945.

Somewhere in the middle of Arizona, we heard the news that changed everything once again. The newscaster on the car radio announced we had dropped the first atom bomb. About five days later, we dropped the second one. That ended the war, effectively. Those two bombs saved thousands of lives . . . and very likely saved mine. Once again, God worked things out for the good.

The Japanese defended the outlying islands with suicidal ferocity. They would have fought to a bitter death defending their homeland. There's no question in my mind about it. If it had come to the point where we had to end the war by invading Japan, we would have paid a terrible price in loss of men, and I likely would have been among them. I'm convinced that the numerical disparity between what we actually lost and what we could have lost is vast. I'm convinced that we killed a lot fewer Japanese with the two atom bombs than we and the Japanese would have lost had we invaded Japan by land. They would not have given up. To my dying day, I will be grateful for the atomic bombs. They ended the war.

I had three or four friends killed in the Pacific theater, people who were instructors in my command at La Junta. From time to time people left the training command and went into combat. I have not gotten over those deaths, and I'm not sure I have forgiven the Japanese. I've come to accept what they did, but I'll never buy a Japanese car. Ever.

B-17s and the Roach Motel

The air base in Lovington didn't have quarters for married personnel, so, once again, we moved into a tourist court. This motel was quite a step down from the La Junta motor court. To our dismay, we discovered the worst thing about the place the first night we were there: roaches! We didn't see them in the daytime, but at night, after we went to bed, when we switched the light back on, we saw roaches everywhere. Ceiling and walls. Beth was not crazy about bugs, and neither am I, but at least I can deal with them. She simply froze up. Those little critters made for a few sleepless nights before I finally put an end to them.

After only two months in Lovington, I was fully qualified to fly the B-17, and if the war hadn't ended, I would have been on my way to the Pacific to drop conventional bombs. Instead, because I had committed to serving for another year, we were sent to Texas for the next ten months, assigned first to Big Spring and then to Midland.

I finally got my orders in May 1946 to travel to Fort Smith, Arkansas, for my separation from the military. That's the way the military does things. They couldn't just send me a letter and let me go home, so I drove to Norman and dropped off Beth and Curtis before going on to Fort Smith alone. My time in the Army Air Force gave me more flying time than I could ever have imagined. Though it was stressful and exhausting, as it was for everyone, my wartime experience laid the groundwork for fifty-seven rewarding and exhilarating years in the sky.

RECALLED: THE STRATEGIC AIR COMMAND

Escape and Evasion

In 1951, during the Korean Conflict, the Air Force recalled me from reserve status to active duty and assigned me to Carswell Air Force Base in Fort Worth, Texas. Carswell was a unit of the Strategic Air Command, whose mission was to defend the US by means of a retaliatory strike against any foreign aggressor.

I had always wanted to fly the large airplanes, and in the Strategic Air Command, I got the opportunity and then some. You can bet I reveled in serving as airplane commander of the largest and arguably the most complicated airplane in the world.

Soon after my arrival at Carswell, we were flown to Peterson Air Force Base in Colorado Springs in a C-124, a troop carrier, to attend E&E School (Escape & Evasion). We ended up at a small encampment somewhere north of Colorado Springs in fairly rough, mountainous terrain at about ten thousand feet.

The escape and evasion exercises consisted of three or four days of instruction at camp, after which they turned us loose for another three days in the wilderness with deceptively simple orders: "You've got to get back to your home base, but there are enemy troops between you and there. Your task is to get home without being apprehended."

This was all part of our preparation for possible capture by real enemy forces if we were shot down. They taught us to avoid villages and stay in the woodlands. For sustenance, they gave us pemmican bars, a mixture of protein and fat, used in Alaska and Canada for survival food. The protein is supposed to keep your muscles active, and the fat gives you the energy you need, but it's practically inedible. Absolutely terrible.

Most people didn't eat the pemmican. We survived on a few candy bars and other snacks we brought along. We made slingshots and killed one squirrel. The numerous beaver dams in the area gave us hope of feasting on fish. We made some nets and shooed the fish until they went out through the opening of the dam, but that only yielded two or three trout, not enough to keep us going.

There were several crews participating in the exercise. I don't recall how many. Possibly a half a dozen or so, which meant there were probably eighty or more participating. Our supervisors butchered a cow they bought from one of the ranchers in the area and gave us each a quarter pound of the lean meat. That's not much. To preserve the beef, we built a little tepee and placed racks in it, made a small fire inside, and smoked the meat to cure it.

I'm afraid I didn't last more than a few days before I was

apprehended. We were surrounded by "the enemy," and when I saw an opening, I took out running up a hill as fast as I could. After running two or three hundred yards at ten thousand feet, my knees buckled. Unused to the altitude and loaded down with heavy gear, my body gave out on me. Completely exhausted, I dropped to the ground and waited for somebody to find me. When they did, I couldn't move. No matter how hard I tried, I couldn't get up and walk. My captors transported me to a prison camp, where I got the chance to practice my evasion techniques during interrogation. Luckily, I never had to rely on my escape and evasion training. I'm sure capture by the Soviets would not have been a pleasant experience.

The B-36 and the Bomb

After our initial training, we returned to Carswell and flew regular practice runs on the B-36, then the largest aircraft in the world. It had ten engines, six reciprocating and four jets, and it was capable of flying higher than the combat ceiling of any jet fighter in the world.

All aircrews were required to experience a simulation of explosive decompression, and one person had to volunteer to lose consciousness in the process. A few of us entered one section of a dual chamber and, after we donned oxygen masks, the technicians reduced the pressure to simulate an airplane altitude of ten thousand feet.

I volunteered to be the guinea pig. Once I took off the mask, a membrane between the chambers ruptured, allowing much of the air in our chamber to flow to the other chamber, which had been emptied of air. The change in pressure was deemed "explosive" because it happened in less than a second, and, in that space of time, took the effective altitude of our chamber from ten thousand feet to thirty-three thousand feet.

The pressure change was startling in itself, but it also produced a fog in the chamber, which, though it lasted only a few seconds, added to the confusion. As the guinea pig, I had to write my name, rank, and serial number as many times as I could before losing consciousness. As you can see from my scribbling that day, I managed to write my ID information twice in the twenty-eight seconds before I passed out. That fit in the predicted range (my note indicates I lasted thirty-two seconds, but I think that's incorrect). They slapped the oxygen mask back on my face, and, unaware I'd lost consciousness for a few seconds, I resumed writing as though nothing had happened.

The Unthinkable Becomes Routine

I served as copilot for my initial time of duty, but later I became the pilot, which meant I commanded the airplane and our fifteen-member crew. We were on call 24/7, and if war had broken out, we would immediately have joined the other crews to retaliate.

The defensive armament of the B-36 consisted of sixteen 20mm cannons. Their weight kept us below an altitude of fifty thousand feet. Sometime after I left active duty, all the cannons except those in the tail were eliminated. They weren't needed, and the weight loss allowed them to fly above fifty-two thousand feet.

The B-36 had two crew compartments, one at the front end and one in the tail. Four bomb bays separated the two compartments. Each of the bomb bay doors operated independently to open or close. The airplane was designed to carry a maximum bomb load of 84,000 pounds. Or we could carry one atom bomb. Later, the plane was modified to carry two. I don't know why you would want to carry two atom bombs. One would destroy everything within a ten-mile radius.

The regular bombs rested on two or four racks attached by

hooks. The bombardier controlled the racks, which were electrically uncoupled to let the bombs drop out. To accommodate the atom bomb in the B-36, the racks in the middle of the forward and adjacent bomb bay were removed. That left one rack on each side to support the atom bomb, which weighed about 9,800 pounds. The encasement was probably a couple thousand pounds. High explosives—7,000 pounds—accounted for most of the rest of the weight.

We had no rockets in those days, only machine guns or cannons. The development of rockets doomed the B-36, which was slow and could only fly up to fifty-two thousand feet. The Russians had faster airplanes. I don't know whether they could fly farther or not, but they had electronic counter measures, which I think were not very successful.

We had an interesting method, called chaff, for evading the enemy radar. Chaff is just like the stuff that flew out of the threshers back on the farm. That's probably where they got the idea. As you'll recall, the threshers whirled the grain around and separated all of the stems and hulls, which were lighter. The grain would fall out one end and the lighter stuff—small particles of seedlings, stems, and seedpods—would flow out the other, and that was called chaff. We dropped a different kind of chaff—very thin, tiny particles of aluminum, like aluminum foil—out of our B-36s and other airplanes to confuse the enemy's radar, which would pick it up. Hopefully. That was one of our lower-tech defense systems.

Our targets were top secret, but Russia was our only enemy. There were at least a hundred, maybe two hundred, B-36s stationed in secret bases around the US. Many were equipped, certified, and ready at a moment's notice to fly to Russia and drop bombs. I'm sure Russia knew that. Only the airplane commander, the navigator and the bombardier knew our exact target. In the event of war, our crew's target would have been on the north side of Moscow.

Fast-forward fifty-two years: Beth and I were on a mission trip to Russia with a large group. We were on a cruise ship from St. Petersburg to Moscow with five doctors and eight nurses on board. The rest of us were there to do street witnessing and give Bibles to all who were interested in cities along the way. We ended our trip in Moscow, where we witnessed and gave away Bibles at a medical clinic, in a school, and on the streets of the city. I didn't realize it right away, but once I looked at a map, I saw that we were in the northwest quadrant of Moscow.

Fifty-two years after my secret missions for SAC, I found myself witnessing for God five miles within the assigned target of my B-36.

I thank God for sparing me from the task of dropping an atom bomb on Moscow or anywhere else. By His grace, instead of wiping out the entire population of this great city, I brought the good news of eternal and abundant life promised by our Lord for all who believed in Him.

THE BRANIFF
YEARS

Safe Landing in Dallas, Texas

I went to work for Braniff Airlines in July 1946, and we settled down in Dallas in a little house on Grove Street near Love Field. It was so close to the airport that about four years later, when the airport expanded, they bought us out. We subsequently purchased a house a mile or so north big enough to accommodate our growing family. We already had Curtis, of course. Our other three children were born in Baylor Hospital in Dallas. Bill arrived in 1949, and in 1954 we had the twins, Rick and Susan.

For the first ten years, I flew the DC-3 as a copilot. Going from copilot to captain involves a checkout procedure to demonstrate to the airline and the Federal Aviation Authority that you're equipped and able to fly captain on an airplane.

Once you pass, you're king of the roost. Most airlines were expanding faster than Braniff, and their new hires checked out in as little as three or four years, but I had to wait much longer.

I reveled in flying airplanes for a living, and when I made captain in 1956, I loved taking complete charge of the plane. But there was a down side. When I first checked out, I had very little control over my schedules. Everybody above me took their pick and I got what was left. I was flying what they call "the south-end schedule" in Texas. Typically I'd go to work at eight in the morning and fly to Houston. I'd wait there a while before flying on to San Antonio, then Brownsville, and back to San Antonio, where I'd spend the night. The next day, I might fly to Dallas and repeat the whole thing all over again. I'd spend three or four days shuttling around South Texas.

The schedule was rough, especially for a guy with a young family, but it was a steady job, and I thought I had a good future with Braniff. By 1959, we were financially stable enough to take out a pretty good size loan on a new house—$35,000. We bought a wooded acre in Lakewood not far from Mount Vernon, the H. L. Hunt place overlooking the lake. I like to say we lived about $15 million west of H. L. Hunt's place.

Our builder was an architect, and he helped me design the house. We had 3,800 square feet, enough room for our four kids, my mother-in-law, and a dog. The kids loved playing outside, and they had plenty of space to run around with all their friends in the neighborhood.

Thanks to Braniff, I was able to provide a very nice life for my family, but one of my biggest regrets is that I did not spend enough time with my children. I guess because I learned it all on my own, I thought they could too, and that's a pretty narrow-minded attitude. I should have been there more for them. I was always available to help our kids with schoolwork, but I should have spent more time showing them how to do things, how to make things, how to put things together, and how to play. Unfortunately, I didn't.

It didn't help that I was away from home every weekend, leaving Beth to parent alone. I especially didn't like to be away in the summers, when the kids were out of school all day. Plus, I was trying to teach a Sunday school class in my church, and my schedule didn't really allow that either. Family and church were number one with me, so after about three or four years as a captain, I made a career change. I decided, hey, this is no way to live, and I returned to copiloting. It was a deliberate, purposeful decision that supported my commitment to God and family.

Because of my seniority, as top copilot I made about as much as the bottom captain, and I practically had first choice of all the schedules. I often flew freighters on turnarounds to Chicago or New York, which meant I'd leave Dallas around ten o'clock at night and return eight hours later. I was only away from home about twelve nights in three and a half years. Beth always contradicted me on this. She said, "Yeah, but some of those nights you didn't get home until three in the morning." True, but it was a big improvement. I got to be the kind of dad I never had, the kind of dad every child deserves. And I was able to devote myself seriously to our church, which meant a lot to me.

Though it was the right decision for my family, I have to admit copiloting was a comedown. It's one thing to be in the left seat and quite another to occupy the right seat. There's a lot more prestige in being called captain and wearing four stripes on your sleeve. I stayed with copiloting about three and a half years. Then, I had the opportunity to become captain on the Boeing 727, and I couldn't resist.

Captain of My Ship

The Boeing 727 is a three-engine, mid-size aircraft that accommodates 149 to 189 passengers as well as a lot of cargo. It was pretty much the standard airplane for the Braniff fleet. We probably had more 727s than all other models combined. We had some DC-8s and some Boeing 707s, which were good airplanes to fly, but the 727 was a great airplane, and I enjoyed flying it for nine years.

Just like a ship captain on the ocean, when you're in the air, you're in complete command. You can do anything you want to, but you have to answer to the authorities once you bring that airplane back to the gate. If you've taken extraordinary measures to deal with a situation, if you've deviated from any kind of rule, you have to be prepared to justify it. It's a great feeling, but it's a very, very great responsibility as well.

Whenever I got a new copilot, once he had checked out, and we were seated in the cockpit side by side, I'd say to him, "There's one thing you need to learn about being a copilot with me. This half of the airplane, from the middle to the left window, this half is mine." Then I'd stretch my arm across him and touch the window on his right. "This half is ours."

We were usually paired with one copilot for a full month. We would bid our schedules for the coming month and the copilots would bid, and we'd end up paired. One month I was paired with a copilot named Wilbur! On every flight that month, I was sorely tempted to get on the PA system and tell the passengers, "Today you're flying with Orville and Wilbur." I wish I had done it. I dearly wish I had. Now you know one of the few regrets of my life.

As captain I sometimes attended to details that had nothing to do with piloting the plane. For instance, if the flight attendant thought an unruly passenger needed attention, I had to take care of the situation. I only had to take one passenger off one of my airplanes in my whole career. I was flying out of Amarillo going to Memphis, and we had not yet taken off. The head flight attendant came into the cockpit and said, "I've got a passenger I can't deal with." We had just taxied out, and we were ready to run up the engines and do a final check before takeoff. I left the copilot with the brake set and went back to the cabin.

"He's unruly, and I don't think I want him on my airplane," the flight attendant said.

The problem passenger was obviously drunk and belligerent, so I told him to sit down. I guess my uniform got his attention, because he obeyed. Nevertheless, I didn't want to take the chance he'd go berserk up in the air, so we taxied back to the terminal and got him off the plane. That's the only problem I ever had with a passenger in my whole career. Thank the Lord.

* * * I flew for Braniff for thirty-one years, and I would have continued much longer, but at that time airline pilots were required to retire at age sixty. I wasn't nearly ready to quit, but rules are rules, and in 1977, reluctantly, I ended my commercial flying career. I've been retired for nearly forty years—nine years longer than I flew for Braniff. I resented the forced retirement to a degree, but you can't let resentment run your life. You take what's doled out, what's inescapable, and you deal with it. I learned that lesson way back in Okemah when I fell out of the tree and got a whipping from my dad. Sometimes life is unfair, but you move on to better days.

It didn't take long for a silver lining to show up. My retirement freed me for something much more important. No doubt God had a hand in the next chapter, as He did in all the chapters of my life.

FLYING FOR GOD

A Prayer for Guidance

The most dramatic answer to my prayers came after my retirement from Braniff. I was a passenger, winging toward Dallas/Fort Worth airport from Waxhaw, North Carolina, where I had attended a board meeting of JAARS (Jungle Aviation and Radio Service, a service arm of Wycliffe Bible Translators). I had not flown as a pilot in more than six months, and, though I had been ferrying airplanes for JAARS since 1966, I had not been called upon for nearly a year. Self-doubt crept in: Perhaps the FAA rule makers were right. Maybe I was too old to fly a plane.

Why, then, did I feel so uncomfortable riding in the rear? My mind entertained the notion of quitting, but my instinct was telling me otherwise. The bureaucrats decreed an airline pilot must stop flying at age sixty, but that couldn't prevent me from continuing to ferry small aircraft for JAARS or taking Beth and the family on pleasure trips.

If I wanted to continue flying, the rules on piloting were clear: I could not fly with passengers until I had been given a check ride or made three takeoffs and landings in the type of plane that I wanted to fly. It seemed that time was moving as swiftly as the Douglas DC-8 that now carried me home.

At the familiar sound of the chime, I looked up at the "Fasten Seat Belt" sign and wondered if the message was more significant than the mere command to buckle up for a landing. Was the Lord telling me it was time to hang it up and take a seat in the rear of the plane? As the pilot began our descent, I began to talk to God in a very personal way. "Is that what you are saying, God? Is it time to let flying go?" For some reason I added, "God, please let me know right away." Until then, I had seldom, if ever, been that demanding of God. But after sixty years of experience in prayer, I believed—and still believe—that's the way God wants us to talk to Him.

The next morning, less than twelve hours after my prayer, the telephone rang. My good friend, Dr. Bert Lyles, had a request. "Orville, could you possibly fly a new Cessna Golden Eagle to Leeds, England, as a personal favor to me? Expenses paid, of course," he said. "From there, you can ferry a twin-engine Piper Navajo back to Dallas."

It wasn't God—but Bert's voice sure enough carried a message from God. I had my answer, right away.

I told Bert I'd be happy to do it, and he said he would call me by eight o'clock the next morning to set things up.

At nine o'clock the next morning, I still hadn't heard back from Bert, but I did get a call from Doyle Combs, someone I'd never met. "Orville, I'm in a great predicament," he said. "I hope you can help me out." He had planned a dental mission trip to Mexico set to depart at noon that day, and his pilot had backed out of the trip. Although Doyle was a pilot, he said he didn't feel qualified to fly into Mexico. He desperately wanted to get his pastor and a dentist to Los Piedritos, a tiny village just across the border.

"Could you possibly fly us in my Cherokee 6? You'd leave at noon and come back tomorrow," he said. I told him I was waiting for confirmation on a ferry to England. "I'll give him another hour to call me," I said. "If I don't hear from him, I'll fly your people to Mexico."

Two flying opportunities within twenty-four hours! God was indeed answering my prayer right away! When I didn't hear from Bert, I arranged to meet Doyle and get qualified to fly passengers. Bert called right after I hung up. "No problem," he said. "We can delay our trip for a couple of days."

Three hours later I was on the way to Mexico with Doyle and his team. We spent a night in Cuidad Acuña, where we cleared customs. The next morning I flew west over miles of northern Mexico's empty, arid land to the little town of Los Piedritos.

Doyle and his pastor, Dr. Jerry Poteet, witnessed to the long lines of people waiting for treatment. Dr. Russell Jenkins pulled about thirty-five teeth and provided painkillers and antibiotics, which was about all he could do in the limited time available. They put me to work sterilizing the dental instruments. By midnight, I had flown my first post-retirement mission trip, and we were back in Dallas in our comfortable homes.

The following morning Bert and I caught a Braniff flight to Wichita, Kansas, and picked up a beautiful new Cessna 421 Golden Eagle. I flew it to Dallas, and the next day I took off for Leeds, spending nights in Bangor, Maine, and Reykjavik, Iceland, on the way.

I checked out in the Navajo I needed to fly back to Dallas, and in three days I was back home. I had flown eighty-five hours—a normal month's workload for a commercial airline pilot—in eleven days!

I had asked God to tell me what to do next, and He set His answer in motion with head-swimming speed. I firmly believe that God not only wants the very best for us, but also that He wants us to ask it of Him. For the next seventeen years, I flew airplanes in the service of my Lord, facing great challenges as well as moments of unspeakable joy. I only had to ask and it was given.

JAARS: Jungle Aviation and Radio Service

I met William Cameron "Uncle Cam" Townsend, the founder of Wycliffe Bible Translators, in 1965. He impressed me with the work he was doing, and I asked him if I could help the organization out in some way. He didn't waste any time putting me on a project called the #2 Helio Courier to Colombia. The Helio Courier, manufactured in Pittsburg, Kansas, from 1954 to 1974, is still popular among missionaries for flying into rough jungle airstrips. The six-passenger, single-engine STOL (short takeoff and landing) aircraft is perfect for flying in and out of very short jungle airstrips by heavily loaded aircraft. Wycliffe had one lined up for their Colombia mission, and though it was ready to go, it wasn't paid for. With friends and relatives, we raised the money to pay it off in short order, and Uncle Cam asked me to ferry it to Bogota. I'm not sure I could have imagined then that this would be the first of forty-one flights for Wycliffe and four for Southern Baptists evenly divided between South America, Africa, and Southeast Asia.

After World War II, worldwide missionary activity increased dramatically. But the lack of adequate and safe ground transport and commercial aviation services posed a great handicap to the spreading of the Gospels. The creation of missionary aviation filled the need with organizations like Jungle Aviation and Radio Service. The acronym, JAARS, came into use when aviation and radio no longer represented the paramount service needs of Wycliffe Bible Translators. At its peak, JAARS had more than sixty-five aircraft in service worldwide. Today JAARS also ministers in ground transportation, water transportation, computers, and other important areas providing assistance to the missions.

The largest of the missionary support organizations is still Missionary Aviation Fellowship (MAF) with more than 120 aircraft in their service as of a few years ago. There are many other groups that have aviation needs, and some of them have their own flying arm (the Catholic's Wings of Hope, for example), while others depend on MAF, JAARS, and others for help.

Christian airline pilots offer their services to ferry aircraft for these various mission groups. Some help with the expenses of the flights in addition to donating their time. We pilots almost always obtain free or reduced fares on commercial airlines to get back home. As these flight services increased, it became clear that cooperation and support among these various groups was essential. Seven of us formed MAFS: Missionary Aircraft Ferry Service, which coordinates the services and provides information fellowship. Captain Robert Burdick, a senior United Airlines captain, led the effort and suggested Psalms 139: 9–10 for our motto:

"If I ride the morning winds to the farthest oceans, even there your hand will guide me, your strength support me."

Before GPS: Flying by the Seat of Our Pants

In the early days, lack of directional guidance during flights over water and in many remote jungle areas posed one of the greatest challenges missionary aviation faced. Many of the countries we served did not have adequate radio navigation facilities, and that hampered the task of ferrying airplanes to these parts of the world. In some areas a system called LO-RAN (long-range radio navigation) was a help, but for most of our flying there was a distinct need for an accurate world navigation system. Imagine one of our ferry pilots over the Pacific Ocean in bad weather, with dwindling fuel supplies, looking for a tiny dot of an island whose only radio transmitter is off the air. Believe me—it happened.

Then, in 1989, the US government placed satellites with radio signals (Global Positioning Systems [GPS]) into orbit several hundred miles above the earth. Now even a small handheld unit (my first aviation GPS was nearly one cubic foot!) can tune in three or more of these satellites that are in line-of-sight at any time, and, with atomic clocks accurate to billionths of a second, determine a position anywhere on Earth.

Along with position information, GPS provides accurate ground speed, wind drift, and altitude readouts. On one of my last ferry flights, from North Carolina to Nairobi, the DC-3 had GPS interfaced with our fuel gauges and the fuel flow meter. This enabled us to continually monitor our calculated fuel remaining at the end of the flight. GPS has revolutionized long-range flying and made it safer, more economical, and a great deal more enjoyable.

I find further reassurance in this advanced technology that God is with us always. The Holy Spirit whispered these words in King David's ear twenty-five hundred years before GPS satellites came into use: "If I ride the morning winds to the farthest oceans, even there your hand will guide me, your strength support me" (Psalms 139:9). God knew then that far in the future, we ferry pilots would feel reassured by His presence. Through modern technology, He watches over us, guides us, and supports us as we fly over the oceans in His service.

Into the Glory

The sequel to my first flight for JAARS brought me together with Jamie Buckingham, a Christian author who had been asked to write a book about JAARS and the part aviation played in the missions of Wycliffe Bible Translation. Jamie wanted to ride with me to Colombia and travel from there to other countries in South America, where Wycliffe Bible Translators and JAARS were having the greatest impact.

Jamie had achieved some fame with the release of his first book, Run Baby Run, the story of Nicky Cruz, a young New York City gang leader who had become a Christian and a strong witness to his former associates. Speculation was rife with the tongue-in-cheek suggestion that the new book would be titled *Fly Baby Fly*.

Jamie did travel with me to Colombia and to other countries, and I believe I had a little bit to do with the title of the book he wrote about JAARS. He told the story in the preface of his book. Here is an excerpt:

> Our single-engine plane was over the broad expanse of the blue Caribbean Sea. Behind us was Kingston, Jamaica, our last fuel stop until we touched down on the South American continent—far over the southern horizon.
>
> We climbed to eleven thousand feet in order to ride the tops of the white, fluffy clouds that hung suspended between us and the blue-green water two miles below.
>
> Orville Rogers, an off-duty jet pilot for Braniff Airlines, was in the left-hand seat of our small plane. I was beside him, uncomfortable in my life jacket, making my third trip to the Amazon jungle. We were delivering the plane to a small group of jungle pilots—Jungle Aviation and Radio Service (JAARS). Backed up by mechanics and radio per-

sonnel, they were flying Bible translators into the most remote sections of the earth.

Orville nodded out the window.

"Look below."

There, skimming along on the tops of the clouds, was
the shadow of our tiny plane. It was surrounded by a
bright, almost golden halo.

"That halo often becomes a circular rainbow," Orville
said. "It's called the pilots' halo."

I stared down, fascinated by the little shadow speeding
along on the tops of the fleecy clouds.

"Airline pilots refer to that ring of light as the glory,"
Orville said softly, his voice barely distinguishable over
the roaring engine in front of us. "Sometimes as we start
our descent toward the clouds, that circle of light grows
intensely brighter, and the moment the plane and shadow
converge in the cloud, there's a brilliant burst of light. We
call it flying into the glory."

I sat for a long time, looking down at the shadow,
clouds, and water far below. I remembered, from my childhood days in Sunday school, the angels who appeared after
Jesus was caught up into a cloud. "So shall He return again
in all His glory," they said.

My mind raced ahead to where I would be tomorrow—
in the Amazon jungle. There my pilot friends were risk-
ing—even giving—their lives, that the Bible-less tribes of
the world might read that wonderful promise in their own
language. These pilots, too, were flying into the glory. Only
they weren't descending, they were climbing on course.[2]

* * *

I had picked up Jamie at Fort Lauderdale, where he was
the pastor of an independent church, and we had flown on

---

2. Jamie Buckingham, *Into the Glory*. (Plainfield, NJ: Logos International,
1974).

to Miami to spend the night. After we put the airplane to bed and filed a flight plan for the next day, we checked into a motel for some sleep. (If you can call five hours, *some*. My friend Bernie May once remarked after a short night in my house, "It certainly does not take long to spend the night at your home.")

During our prayers before retiring, I asked for some good rest and for God's blessing on the next day's flight. I told Jamie that I never asked God to give me good weather on my ferry flights, but to give me wisdom to deal with whatever weather He sent.

"Well, that's all right for you, but I'm going to pray for good weather," he replied.

I don't know how much influence Jamie had with the Lord, but we did have good weather all the way to Bogota.

There was, however, a time of grave concern. The first part of our climb out from Miami was routine, but as we were climbing to fifteen thousand feet, our assigned cruising altitude, the engine oil pressure plunged toward the red line. Without adequate oil pressure the engine will soon begin to develop friction in the moving parts, and that will inevitably destroy the engine. Oil-pressure loss strikes fear into the heart of any pilot, especially over water. It's right up there with a fire on board and a midair collision. I decided to climb just a bit more to get a better picture of the situation, and the pressure dropped right down to the red line. Without hesitation, I made a 180-degree turn and headed back to Miami.

Soon after we began the descent, the oil pressure rose toward the normal range. Very odd, I thought. That had never happened before, and in my thirty-eight-thousand-plus hours of flying, it never happened to me again. The pressure continued to rise as I descended. My next decision was not without risk. I called air traffic control and informed them my problem had resolved. I asked if our flight plan could be reinstated. With an affirmative from the tower, we continued on to Kingston without further incident. You can be sure I paid close attention to the oil pressure all the way. I think the oil-pressure drop must have been related to the altitude change. When we arrived in Bogota I made sure that the pilots in Colombia were made aware of this very odd aberration.

I flew into the glory for nineteen more years after God's decisive answer to my prayer. I was grateful to Him for the many opportunities I had to serve Him and the missionaries who sacrificed so much to spread the message of God's love.

Early Years

My parents on their honeymoon. This is the only photo I have of my father.

Grandmother Mary Johnston, my sister Veva, me, and my mother.

The Johnston family, 1935. Front row: Grandfather Reuben Jefferson and Grandmother Mary. Back row: Dan, Votie, Bill, Lilly, and Ralph

Beth and I on our wedding day in La Junta, Colorado, June 3, 1943

The happy bride and groom with Beth's sister Ruth, who was her maid of honor, and my best man, Edward Grossheider.

Flight training in 1941 at Lindbergh Field in the Ryan PT22.

Flight training in 1940 in Ft. Worth, before I became a cadet.

I was a proud cadet in 1941 at Lindbergh Field, just before Pearl Harbor.

Second Lieutenant Orville Rogers, 1942.

During the Korean Conflict, I flew the B-36, the world's largest airplane at the time, on secret practice missions for the Strategic Air Command.

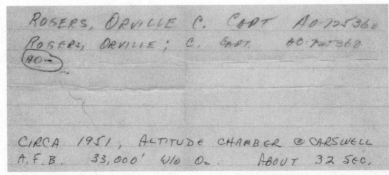

I kept the note on which I wrote my name and serial number for the oxygen deprivation test during B-36 training at Carswell AFB. The circled scribble on line 3 shows when I passed out.

B-36 engineer's instruments.

B-36 Pilot's instruments

In command of a Convair 340 for Braniff.

```
                    FERRY FLIGHT CHECK LIST

                          Personal
     1. Passport                    7. Prescription glasses & spa⌐
     2. Visas                       8. Sunglasses
     3. Health Card
     4. Travelers Checks
     5. Cash
     6. Credit cards


                          Aircraft
AK.  1. FAA ferry permit            26. Disinfectant spray (⌐
     2. Aircraft registration certificate
Ferry 3. Airworthiness certificate
     4. Radio license
     5. Aircraft manual
     6. Aircraft & Engine Logs
     7. International Flight Information Manual
     8. Enroute Radio Facilities Charts
     9. Approach Plates
    10. VFR charts
    11. Export papers
    12. Landing & overflight permits
    13. Insurance certificate
    14. Fuel contracts
    15. International Flight plans
    16. General Declaration Forms
    17. Survival gear
    18. Food & water for flight
    19. First Aid Kit
    20. Duplicate keys for doors & ignition
    21. Flashlights & penlight
    22. Two Thermos - Water & Coffee
    23. Plastic Bottle for urinal
    24. Handi-wipes
    25. Litter bags
```

I used this checklist to prepare for every ferry flight.

Missionary Ferry Flights

Two Helio Couriers I delivered to Liberia four years apart. I am wearing a hat given to me by a tribal chief.

Ferry flight to Papua New Guinea

This Cessna 206 bound for Burkina Faso is one of the many planes I ferried.

I ferried the overhauled Curtis Rogers to Belem, Brazil in 1983. The Curtis Rogers, Friend of Bethany was named in honor of Orville and Beth's son Curtis who was killed in the Vietnam War on November 18, 1970.

Beth and I flew the Curtis Rogers, a Cessna 206, to Belem, Brazil for the Wycliffe mission in 1973.

The Curtis Rogers on its way to Belém, Brazil, 1973.
Photo credit: Mike Rupp

After ferrying this airplane to Ukarumpa with Bob Burdick (second from left) in 1980, I handed the keys to Karl Franklin (far right) as a Stu Nelson offered up a prayer of thanks.

With two of my dearest friends, Bernie May (left) and Bob Burdick (center) before a flight to Switzerland.

Ready for a seventy-two-hour ferry flight to Indonesia. A special navigation radio is mounted on top of the instrument panel.

Many ferry flights required extra fuel tanks, which took up the entire back of the plane.

End of a two-mile run at Cooper Aerobics Center, 2009.

I'm a world champion runner and I have the medals to prove it!
Photo credit: Don Michel

Family

With my two sisters—Veva on the left and Sandra on the right.

Curtis at Marine Corps training in Pensacola, Florida, 1968.

Proud father of sons Rick (left) and Bill (right).

My dear daughter, Susan.

Granddaughter Elizabeth welcomed me home from Honor Flight to Washington, D.C. circa 2011.

The grandchildren at Mackinac Island family reunion, July 2014: Nina, Shannon, Sarah Beth, Elizabeth, Jessica, Brad, Patrick, Michael, Will, Steven, Curtis, Chris, Neal

Rogers Family Reunion at Mackinac Island, July 2014.
Front Row: Evie, her mother Shannon, Ryan, Ellie and her grandmother Melanie, Orville, Susan with Caleb, Jane with Madison
Back Row: Patrick holding Lillie, Brad holding Bradley, Elizabeth holding Will, Bill, Chris, Jennifer, Jessica holding Esther, Neal, Ken, Michael, Nina, Will, Rick, Steven, Sarah Beth, Curtis

Family Reunion in Vermont

Rogers Family Reunion in Kenya, July 2016.
Front Row: Guide, Steven, Lillie, Curtis, Ellie, Nina, Sarah Beth, Brad, Evie, Will, Elizabeth, Ryan, Jennifer, Madison, Caleb
Back Row: Shannon, Melanine, Guide, Will, Jane, Patrick, Guide, Orville, Guide, Bill, Guide, Guide holding Bradley, Steven, Guide, Rick, Chris holding Hunter, Ken, Susan

Our first formal portrait, taken soon after our wedding day. Sixty years later, we were still devoted to one another and celebrating the anniversary of that blessed day.

With Chuck Yeager, WWII flying ace.

At Nike headquarters with Nike president of Innovation, Tom Clarke (Sandra's son-in-law), and Alberto Salazar, world-famous long-distance runner and coach of the Nike Oregon Project.

Surrounded by champions: Former Texas governor Rick Perry (fourth from left), Ken Cooper (first on left), and I talk running with two of the greatest, Bill Rodgers (second from left) and Frank Shorter (right). Longtime friends Rodgers and Shorter have each run over 190,000 miles.

Dr. Cooper and I posed with the Kenneth Cooper Prize for Aerobic Leadership awarded to me by the Tyler Cup Foundation, 2008.

ORVILLE ROGERS
98, running, Dallas

At age 50, Rogers' only activity was an occasional game of racquetball or handball. Then he picked up Kenneth Cooper's *Aerobics*, a best-selling book about running, and hit the road the next day. "I ran a mile very slowly," he says. Since then, he has logged 42,000 miles, including five marathons. "But I didn't get into serious competitions until I was 90," he says. "I looked up the records and thought I could [beat] them. I set world records for one mile and 800 meters in my age group, 90 to 94."

Rogers, who runs three times a week followed by 45 minutes of strength training, will miss the outdoor nationals this year because he's going on an African safari. But he'll compete at the indoor nationals next March.

Tip: "Every scientific study shows that if you exercise, you live longer. That's the icing on the cake. Your health is the incentive. The enjoyment comes after that."

Parade magazine took note of my long running career in their Olympics issue in 2016.

EVERY DAY AND EVERYWHERE, GOD WATCHES OVER ME

I do not believe in an angry, disinterested God. My God is a loving Father who is there to guide me along the path He has chosen for me. I discover my path in this earthly existence by listening to God, and I ask Him to watch over me and help me as I carry out His will. Though I have encountered plenty of rough spots on the trail, God has never failed me.

Fifty-seven years of flying provided numerous graphic examples of God's intervention for good in my life. After He ushered me toward a career in flight, God appeared again and again to keep me alive and flying in his service.

Close Calls and One Test of Faith

One early JAARS ferry flight brought me together with my friend Bob Burdick, a United Airlines pilot and long-time JAARS pilot. We were scheduled to fly a couple of Cessna 206s to Yarinacocha, an outpost deep in the rainforest that serves as the operations base for Wycliffe Bible Translators in Peru. Bob picked up his plane in Chicago, and I flew from Dallas to Waxhaw for mine. I began the return trip in the Cessna after dark and stopped for the night in Jackson, Mississippi, due to stormy weather in Dallas.

The next day, as I flew over Louisiana, I noticed the oil pressure dropping. I saw nothing but treetops all the way to the horizon—not a good place for a forced landing. Though the steady drop continued, I decided I could make it to Tyler in East Texas.

In Tyler, I taxied to a fixed base operator (FBO), and their mechanics flushed out the oil system and ran up the engine to several power settings. To my surprise, the pressure was completely normal. We put our heads together and concluded a bit of metal or something had gotten under the pressure-relief valve seat. During the flight, it had worked its way deeper and deeper, which allowed increasing amounts of engine oil to flow back to the oil tank, bypassing the engine parts it should have been lubricating.

With that mystery solved, I flew on to Dallas to pick up Beth, and we made it to Yarinacocha without further incident. Though it was an enjoyable trip, especially with Beth on board, I couldn't help thinking how easily it could have gone wrong: If the metal chip had waited another few flying hours, we would have been over rainforests in Central and South America—a much worse situation for a forced landing than the semitropical forests of Louisiana. Worse, if the pressure-relief valve had failed during a JAARS flight in the jungles of Peru, that would have been a real disaster.

Bob and I returned to South America many times, but we avoided the mainland route, preferring to fly over Cuba and Jamaica and on to Colombia or Brazil over open water. A member of our Air and Sea Rescue unit in Corpus Christi, Texas, once told me, "If you ever have to ditch in the Gulf or our area of the Atlantic and can send a distress signal, we'll find you."

A look at forced landings in a rain forest present a bleak picture. When a Peruvian airliner went down in the jungle near Pucallpa, Peru, several days of air reconnaissance yielded no sign of the airliner, and the rescue effort was discontinued. The tops of the trees simply closed in over the remains of the plane. The only survivor of the crash, a female passenger, walked miles through dense, nearly impassable undergrowth to an outpost and directed rescuers to the wreckage.

* * *

Bob Burdick and I faced a variety of challenges together in our flights for JAARS. Burdick was a droll man, and very funny. He liked to say, "These ferry flights are a piece of cake—after they're over." Most of my flights—at least three-quarters—had a weather or mechanical problem or both. And there was often a difficulty with customs and immigration. It was never a piece of cake.

Once we were called upon to ferry a Cessna 206 from Waxhaw to Ukarumpa in Papua New Guinea, and we decided to depart from Santa Barbara, a fairly small airport right on the California coast. We usually tried to schedule a long flight over land before a long one over an ocean in order to get a good check on the fuel and oil consumption as well as the heavy aircraft's performance for its first long flight over water. When we checked the plane before takeoff at Santa Barbara, we took the engine cowling completely off to examine the engine thoroughly, as we always did before an overwater flight. It's a good thing we did, because we found a loose belt on the generator that probably would have failed after a few hours of flying time.

The next day we taxied out to the takeoff runway, pausing there to give the last check of the engine RPM, the ignition system, and other details. I was flying left seat on the first leg. The final check indicated we were okay to go, and we received our clearance from the tower: "Cessna November 6589, behind the landing United DC-8, you are cleared into position and hold."

I advanced the throttle to move onto the runway, and the plane did not move. We were very heavy with all the extra fuel, which made it harder to get going, so I moved the throttle well up on the quadrant. But even with nearly full power, the plane still did not move. I pulled back the throttle, and Bob and I tried to figure out what could be wrong. Then I looked out my window and saw we had a flat tire!

I could see the pointed end of a nail protruding from the sidewall, which meant the head was inside the casing. Very, very strange. The plane had flown about fifty hours since leaving the factory. We finally concluded that the worker who assembled the tire and tube must have put a nail inside the casing. After tumbling around in there for all those takeoffs and landings, its point finally penetrated the casing and its head wore through the tube, causing our flat.

The FBO sent out a tug with a temporary wheel and put it on the landing gear so we could taxi back to the repair station. They didn't have a replacement tube, so we had to drive to the Los Angeles area to find one. To add insult to injury, by the time we got the tire fixed, it was too late to take off.

Neither Bob nor I minded the series of delays. On the contrary, we felt the presence of God's protecting hand. If the tire had gone flat just a few minutes later, we would have been rolling down the runway at sixty or more miles per hour. We had nearly two hundred gallons of high-octane fuel in a tank behind us in the cabin and another one hundred or so in the wing tanks. The crash would have instantly turned the airplane into a ball of flames.

* * *

Bob Burdick and I teamed up once again to ferry a twin-engine Aero Commander to the Philippines. The flights from Waxhaw to Oakland and on to Honolulu were routine. Then, on Sunday morning, when we attempted to start the left engine for the leg to Majuro, the next refueling stop, the electric-driven fuel pump didn't work properly. We could hear it grinding, and the gauge showed the fuel pressure rising to only about half the normal value. It was Sunday morning. With no mechanic on duty until the next day, Bob and I put our heads together.

Possible failure of the engine-driven fuel pump in flight concerned us. The carburetor needed fuel pressure to operate properly, and if the fuel pump failed on the way to Majuro, the engine would lose all power unless the back-up electric pump was producing enough power to supply the carburetor. We considered the situation carefully and decided that if the electric pump could supply enough fuel to start the engine, we would continue our trip, knowing that if the electric pump failed completely in Majuro, we would be stuck there waiting for a substitute pump and a mechanic to replace it.

We tried the engine-start and managed to get just enough fuel pressure to get it to kick off. On the flights to Majuro and Guam, we had no further problems restarting. In Manila, while we were unloading our luggage and the spare parts for the plane, the JAARS mechanic took the pump off and disassembled it. He showed us an "O" ring (the seal on the fu-el-pump shaft) had somehow worked itself out of its channel and into the bearing area, where it was grinding itself to pieces every time we turned the switch on. Much more use and it could have been a real problem. Once again, the Lord ensured our safety.

* * *

You might think that with all the close calls and miraculous saves by God, doubt would not creep in. But I'm only human. A ferry to Liberia tested my faith considerably. The mission workload in that country had increased, but a shortage of re-liable roads during rainy season and no roads at all in some areas hampered the missionaries' efforts. They badly needed a second Helio Courier.

The other JAARS pilot and I flew the airplane to Monc-ton, New Brunswick, where the Canadian authorities were to inspect the plane and check out the crew. We were chas-ing a low-pressure system with its associated weather, and it was quite windy when we taxied to the parking place. When I opened the door, a powerful gust tore it out of my hand, snap-ping off the holding bar from the weld.

I sat there a moment, the wind whipping my face, the cold air penetrating my jacket, and a sinful thought popped into my mind: Dear Lord, don't you realize this is a missionary plane going to a place of service in your kingdom's work? Why did this happen, and how can we get this repaired in this tiny town?

I should have asked myself, Why am I not trusting the Lord? While the officials were processing our flight, the other pilot caught a taxi and took the parts to a shop. They quickly discovered the source of our problem—the original weld was a surface weld. It didn't penetrate enough to provide much strength, and that's why the door broke off. If the break had not happened in Moncton, we would have taken the plane on to Liberia, where a break would have been much harder to repair.

* * *

I am certain God is involved in every detail of my life, and that's because I entrust every area of my life to Him. For instance, timing can turn a minor detail into a life or death situation, and who is in charge of timing? God. I was asked at one point to ferry a Helio Courier from Waxhaw, North Carolina, to Liberia. It was to be used by Lutheran Bible Translators to support their efforts in remote areas of Liberia that had poor surface transportation . . . or none at all.

A JAARS pilot named Skip Holmberg was my copilot on this ferry. When I arrived at the JAARS base in Waxhaw, we were informed that the plane had a very small fuel leak in one of the wing tanks. Skip and I agreed that it was not significant enough to delay the trip, but the mechanics refused to give us the go-ahead, saying they did not want to send out a plane that might need repair in the field.

We did another test hop, and when we landed we saw a stain on the fuselage again, where the fuel had dried and left the dye. Another attempt to locate the leak was unsuccessful. Meanwhile, we received a telegram from the engine's manufacturer informing us our plane's engines could have faulty exhaust valves. Upon inspection, the mechanics found the defect, and our plane remained grounded until new valves were installed.

While we waited for the new valves to arrive, the mechanics found the source of the leak, which was completely unrelated to the faulty valves. If they had found the leak before we heard about the faulty valves, we would have taken off and received notice of the faulty valves as we flew over the Atlantic Ocean. Somewhere between Gander in Newfoundland and Santa Maria in the Azores, we would have faced some tough choices. Continue on? Turn back? If we were near the Azores, we would have continued, and if we made it to Santa Maria, we would have been faced with a lengthy and expensive delay while the valves were shipped to us and installed. If one or more of the valves had failed in flight, we would have ditched into the cold North Atlantic waters, and we most certainly would have lost the airplane if not our lives.

Skip and I were ready and willing to take a calculated risk that this was an inconsequential fuel leak. God stepped in via the leak and through the mechanics, who would not let us fly. The timing of that leak was critical. It's the kind of timing that God sets into motion when He is intervening on our behalf.

* * *

Sometimes, God intervenes by manipulating space rather than time. I was the captain on a Braniff flight from Miami to Lima, Peru. I was just entering the pilot's cabin when a mechanic met me with news of a hydraulic leak coming from the nosewheel down-lock cylinder. "A critical part has to be replaced," he said, "and the longer it takes, the longer your flight will be delayed."

He went on to say I could help him hurry along the replacement process by operating the gear-down lever at his command. "I'll talk to you over the interphone from inside the wheel well," he said.

There are moments in every pilot's life that he would like to relive in order to make different decisions. This was one of mine: I agreed to do what the mechanic asked.

Before I could change my mind, I heard his voice crackling over the interphone: "Place the gear lever to the up position."

Already we were starting off on a bad note. That was a very strange request. No pilot wants to do anything that might make the landing gear retract while the plane is on the ground.

"Don't worry," he said. "The hydraulic power is off, the gear locks are in place, and the gear will not come up."

Okay, I thought. He knows what he's doing. We cycled the gear lever up and down a few times.

"Turn on the auxiliary hydraulic pump and place the gear handle up," he said.

Now that was a really strange request. "Are you following approved company procedure?" I asked. "Is this a safe maneuver?"

"I've got it under control," he said.

I turned on the pump and placed the gear handle up, even as my intuition told me not to.

Nothing happened the first time.

"Do it again," he said.

I heard a loud snap. My stomach lurched. The nose of the plane plummeted. Within seconds it came to rest on the nose-wheels.

In those seconds I envisioned that poor man crushed beneath a ton of rubber and steel.

And then I saw him.

He was standing several feet away from his perch on the wheel well, where he had been seconds before, talking to me on the interphone. I pictured the hand of God, plucking him from sure death and placing him uninjured, gently on the tarmac.

I count his survival among the many miracles I have witnessed in my lifetime.

* * *

God takes care of us when we are too befuddled to take

care of ourselves, and that's another form of His constant vigilance over our lives. One of the most stressful experiences of my career as a Braniff pilot happened on the ground. It was 1977, and, once again, I was flying into Lima. The city was experiencing considerable unrest, and a curfew was in effect between sundown and sunrise.

Our flight from New York arrived about eight o'clock, not long after dark. We cleared immigration and customs and got a permit for our transportation to the hotel. The authorities assured us we would not encounter any problems.

Our taxi neared the city center, where cars and trucks and bicycles and hundreds of people crowded the streets. I couldn't see beyond the press of bodies, couldn't hear anything but honking and sirens and shouting. We had been warned about armed guards stationed along the route, and we expected to be stopped for inspection, but that seemed unlikely in the chaos. There were no checkpoints. No barricades. The taxi crawled down the street, stopping every few feet, making its way through the mayhem.

I observed the scene from the back seat, watching it like a movie in slow motion. Anxiety and the heat of the night filled the taxi with thick, heavy air. It was hard to breathe, and sweat soaked my uniform.

A man in soldier's camouflage emerged from the crowd and pointed his automatic weapon at my open window. My heart dropped. He barked a command in Spanish. I didn't understand. The driver kept going, intent on maneuvering the taxi through the chaos. I shouted at him, "Stop!" but he didn't hear and kept right on going.

I clutched his shoulder and shook it. "Stop," I yelled again. Finally he hit the brake. The soldier shoved the barrel of his weapon inside the taxi and leveled it directly at me.

"He is demanding to see our curfew passes," the driver said.

By now we were thoroughly rattled. With trembling hands,

we handed the soldier our papers. Shining his flashlight, he inspected them slowly and carefully, comparing our faces to the pictures. All the while, his gun rested casually on the window frame, aimed at me. Finally, he tossed the papers back, withdrew his weapon, and waved us on. He disappeared into to chaos as swiftly as he had appeared.

A few weeks later, the newspaper reported a Volkswagen bus had failed to stop in a similar situation. Soldiers riddled the bus with bullets and killed several people inside.

The same could so easily have happened to us, yet we were spared. God watched over us that day, just as He has every day of my life.

* * *

In another example of God's vigilance, a generous layman from Mississippi donated a Cessna 210P to the Tanzania mission, where Beth and I had recently served. I picked up the plane and flew it to Iberia, Louisiana, for a STOL modification.

After that modification, I took the airplane to Lancaster, North Carolina, where the extra fuel tanks and the required radios were to be installed for the long over-water flight to Africa. Though it was not legally required, we decided to conduct a one-hundred-hour inspection on the engine and the airframe.

The inspection revealed a hairline crack near the base of one of the six cylinders where it was bolted to the crankcase. Eventually, the crack would have spread and the cylinder would have failed. Had the problem not been detected, this almost certainly would have resulted in complete loss of power, and if the cylinder had ejected from the engine mount, it would have probably damaged the airframe.

In a worst-case scenario, the cylinder would have failed

over the Atlantic Ocean. We would have had to ditch the airplane. The water would have been icy cold, and we would not have lasted long waiting for rescue, two tiny humans bobbing in the deep, wide ocean.

I don't know why we decided to do the inspection, except that I am a big believer in checkups of every kind. Maybe it's the engineer in me. I know how things work, and I know they can stop working for myriad reasons. It's my way of partnering with the Lord, carrying my weight to ensure success in every area of my life.

Reading God's Word and talking daily with Him are forms of checking in, inspecting our spiritual conditions. We have God's promise that He cares for us. Like mechanics care for the airplanes they maintain, so they take to the sky safely, He wants us to do well, to succeed, to accomplish whatever task He has ordained us to do. But we must keep in close fellowship with Him in order to accomplish our God-chosen tasks.

The Flight of the Curtis Rogers

Two ferry trips were especially meaningful to me. The first was on April 27, 1973. Beth and I departed from Dallas in a Cessna 206 named the Curtis Rogers, in remembrance of our son. We were ferrying this winged memorial to Brazil with heavy hearts, but a bittersweet sense of gratitude and accomplishment mingled with our sorrow.

Our eldest shared my name, but we called him Curtis to keep it simple. He also shared my passion for flying, and after graduating from Baylor University, he entered Officer Candidate School and Pilot School in the Marine Corps. In 1968, he earned his wings and became a second lieutenant. In April 1970, he was assigned to Vietnam.

Most of his time in Vietnam, Curtis flew copilot on the CH-46, a twin-engine, heavy duty, troop transport and utility helicopter. Around the end of October, he was promoted to first lieutenant and qualified for airplane commander, which was quite a promotion.

Just a few weeks later, on November 18, his commanding officer dispatched a team to a location behind enemy lines to rescue a squad of Marines, one of whom was wounded and couldn't travel. Curtis served on that team. They were following up on the efforts of another team that had turned back the day before due to bad weather.

These types of rescue missions utilized two helicopters. A high plane served as a gunship to defend the procedure in the event of enemy interference or as an emergency backup. A low plane accomplished the actual rescue. For this mission, Curtis commanded the high plane and Major Tobin commanded the low plane. Major Tobin's helicopter was equipped with a SPIE rig, a cable system that involved a heavy-duty nylon strap fitted with thick metal rings, suspended from a pulley. Whenever they could not land, they would lower the strap through an opening in the floor of the helicopter, down into a clearing. The soldiers below would hook their harnesses onto the strap and the helicopter would transport them to a more suitable landing area. This is probably the most difficult maneuver that a pilot can be called upon to make.

At a refueling stop on the way to the rescue location, Major Tobin noticed a problem with the controls on his helicopter. It may have been a defective collective, which is a stick the pilot maneuvers in order to move the helicopter up and down. Due to the problem with the collective, Major Tobin said he would not be able to perform the rescue mission with his plane, and they transferred the SPIE rig to Curtis's plane. I'm relatively sure that Curtis had worked with a SPIE rig, but probably in ideal conditions, on a clear day, with little or no wind.

With the transfer of the SPIE rig, Curtis's helicopter became the low plane, the rescue ship for the eight-man Marine squad. Due to the bad weather that day, there is a lot of confusion about what happened next.

According to the military accident report, Curtis and his team were able to lower the SPIE rig strap down, and all of the Marines on the ground attached themselves. Curtis would have lowered the plane enough for one man to hook on to the topmost ring. Then he would lift up and another would hook on, until all eight were attached to the strap. The procedure would have been to lift the helicopter high enough for the bottom man to dangle above any obstacles, which means Curtis would have had to climb up quite a bit.

Apparently Curtis accomplished the necessary vertical rise. His plane probably entered a heavy cloud layer, which caused him to lose visibility and orientation from the ground. With eight men dangling from the bottom of the helicopter, Curtis banked in the wrong direction and crashed into a mountainside, a near-vertical wall of rock. The impact killed everyone instantly—Curtis, his men on board, and the soldiers on the strap.

Curtis would have been strongly motivated to carry out his mission even in the worst circumstances. One of the Marine axioms is to never leave a wounded buddy, and if at all possible, bring the dead out when you come out. They made a concerted effort to rescue these eight Marines.

There may have been another incentive to go above and beyond: A Colonel William Leftwich rode in Major Tobin's helicopter to observe the action, which was standard procedure. He was known to be very aggressive, even for a Marine. Many assumed that someday he would likely become the commandant of the Marine Corps. When they transferred the SPIE rig over to Curtis's airplane, Colonel Leftwich moved, too, in order to observe the rescue attempt. Of course, he was killed with all the others.

As Curtis's father and an experienced pilot, I have serious

questions regarding this operation. First and foremost, why was such an inexperienced pilot allowed to perform the most dangerous mission a helicopter could be called upon to perform, in conditions that made it even more challenging?

As I see it, they could have retreated and waited until the next day. A team flew to the site of the crash one day later, and the weather was good. Another option would have been to transfer the SPIE rig from Major Tobin's helicopter to Curtis's, and let Tobin, who was a far more experienced pilot, fly Curtis's plane. That was not standard procedure, but it could have been done, and had it been done, my son would be alive today.

* * *

Beth and I were home on the morning of November 20, 1970, when two Marines came to the door.

As soon as I saw them, I knew.

We picked up Susan and Rick at school and brought them home. Bill was away at school, at Baylor University in Waco. I guess we called him. The rest of that day was just a blur.

We waited all day long to contact Curtis's widow, Marcia, whom he'd married about six months before entering the military. About five or so in the afternoon, we finally found the courage to make the call. Two Marines bearing the terrible news had already visited her.

A few days later Marcia came to Dallas from her home in Nashville, and we had a memorial service at the First Baptist Church. Curtis's body is interred at Restland Memorial Park.

Marcia was terribly affected by Curtis's death, of course. She had gone back to live near her parents and supported herself as a physical therapist while Curtis was in Vietnam. They were scheduled to meet up in Hawaii for an R&R just a few days after his death. She told me they were both looking forward to starting their family during that time together. If they had, one of my grandchildren would be his, and that would be a blessing. Marcia remarried and had four boys, but that has not lessened the connection we have. She and I have stayed close. I still consider her part of the family.

Marcia wanted to know exactly what happened to Curtis, so as I learned the details, I shared them with her. Two of his squadron mates, Paul Wilson and Les Williams, got in touch with us when they came home from Vietnam. Paul lives in Albuquerque and Les is in Colorado. I've seen them both several times over the years, and they were helpful in filling in details about the failed mission, though neither of them participated in it. Both of them were far more experienced pilots than Curtis, and they had some insights into what went wrong. Their viewpoints were very helpful to us, and much of the story I recounted is based on what I learned from them.

I recently sent Marcia a copy of *American Heroes: Grunts, Pilots & "Docs"* by Michael Dan Kullum, which devotes two chapters to Curtis's final mission. In the book Kullum states Curtis was a relatively new pilot in Vietnam, was a relatively inexperienced pilot, and had only been airplane commander about four weeks or less. He adds that the weather described in the accident report was a strong contributing factor. I don't know about Marcia, but, for me, none of these details change the nature of this tragedy. I'm glad to know exactly what happened, but knowing doesn't lessen the grief over the loss of my son.

Life is good, but sometimes it's hard.

* * *

Twenty-one years after Beth and I delivered the Curtis Rogers Cessna 206 to Brazil, I got the chance to ferry it again, this time with a Swiss pilot, Fritz Laufenberger. Back in 1973, Beth and I had shared the cost of the airplane with a church in Phoenix, Arizona. JAARS made good use of it for all those years. In 1994, it was returned to the US for a complete overhaul and a new engine. On October 6, we took off from Waxhaw and flew the rejuvenated Curtis Rogers to Fort Lauderdale. October 7, we landed on Grand Turk. October 8, St. Croix. October 9, Parco, Port of Spain. October 10, Boa Vista, Brazil. October 11, Alta Floresta. And on the seventh day, we landed the airplane in Cuiba, southern Brazil, where it has continued to be put to good use by the missionaries serving there.

I had the honor of flying forty-five airplanes to missions all over the globe. The ferry of the Curtis Rogers to Cuiba, Brazil, was my last.

SERVING MY LORD IN TANZANIA

Ferrying airplanes combined my passion for flight and my passion for God, and believe me: I enjoyed every moment. I have had other opportunities to serve that were not as challenging, perhaps, but extremely rewarding nevertheless. In recent years, I have traveled to Guatemala with my children, and that has been a wonderful experience. The most interesting and gratifying, though, was the extended missionary to Tanzania in 1982, with Beth. I spent thirteen months flying to remote outposts, carrying passengers and making deliveries, and Beth provided the critical ground support that made our mission a success.

By the time Beth and I arrived there, Tanzania had been independent for twenty years. The British left the colonies in 1962, forced out by the Mau Mau. The British had done a great deal for Tanganyika, the name of the territory before independence. They left a good road structure in place—what we'd call farm to market roads—as well as a telephone system, streets, sewage systems, and utilities. After independence, Tanganyika became a socialist state. The resulting government controls caused scarcities in almost all categories. The deterioration of the infrastructure we witnessed was remarkable.

For instance, basic necessities had become scarce or non-existent. We saw a toiletry item for sale one time. I think it was hand soap. You could not buy toilet paper, paper towels, shampoo, toothpaste, or toothbrushes. In my view, that's emblematic of socialism's failure.

Winston Churchill said it most eloquently: "The inherent vice of capitalism is the unequal sharing of blessings; the inherent virtue of socialism is the equal sharing of miseries." I don't deny that socialism has its appeals—everybody working together and sharing. There's a lot of good in that concept. Unfortunately, it doesn't work. People have no incentive to work harder when it's not for their own benefit. If they're paid by the state, they just give their minimum effort. Nothing they can do will help them advance in their careers. In a socialist state, where there's no competition to keep prices low, the state puts a lid on prices and wages. Scarcity is the natural result.

More serious than the shortage of toiletries was the difficulty we had in finding aviation gas. In Tanzania, we often couldn't buy enough, even though it would have been quite profitable for the government to make it available. They could have imported avgas from the Near East and sold it at a good profit. But they couldn't do it efficiently, and we ran out once in a while. I tried my best to stockpile some in jerry cans, and we had a bowser—a small trailer on wheels with a tank on it. You could wheel it out to the airplane to refuel. I kept substantial storage of avgas at the backcountry strips where there just wasn't any gas to be found. I'd buy those jerry cans and fill them full of avgas and fly them to the remote stations and store them there. If I hadn't done that, there would have been plenty of times that I would not have had enough gas to return to our home base at Dar es Salaam.

Jungle Pilot

Beth and I arrived in Tanzania in June and settled into one of the two or three houses in Dar es Salaam owned by the Baptist Mission. They furnished us with a car, too. We just had to buy our own food and gasoline. We had a nice three-bedroom house with a small den, a full kitchen, and an electric washing machine.

Though Tanzania was relatively calm when we got there, a contingent of Marines were based in Dar es Salaam, charged with defense of the American consulate. Their presence might have indicated a threat, but we didn't have any sense of feeling unsafe. Soon after we arrived, we were invited to the American ambassador's beach house for a Fourth of July celebration, and we had a rare opportunity to enjoy an all-American cookout. In the year that followed, those foods from home became a distant memory.

Tanzania is bigger than Texas, and we only had one pilot serving the mission at any given time. Consequently, the airplane's speed was important. I had a Cessna 210, a high-wing, retractable-gear, six-passenger airplane. We had a turbo supercharger in it, which means we could fly up high and go fast. I loved that airplane. I flew freight, mail, anything the missionaries wanted me to. There were about fifteen airports in the country suitable to fly into, five of them in the larger cities. The rest were just grassy or rocky strips. The only way some of those rural stations could get serviced promptly was by air. The roads and railroads were totally inadequate, but the English had put in rudimentary airstrips, and they were still maintained to a degree.

One of my main jobs involved flying visiting dignitaries in

and out. Tanzania did not have very good airline service, so, most of the time, visitors landed in Nairobi, Kenya, a three-hour flight from Dar es Salaam. I'd pick them up there and fly them to Dar es Salaam and on to outlying stations. At the end of their tour a week or two later, I'd take them back to Nairobi for their trip back home.

Another of my principal duties, and the most enjoyable, was flying the missionary kids to school. Some of them attended a school in Dar es Salaam, but it was not nearly as good as Rift Valley Academy, a strict, scholarly, private school on the outskirts of Nairobi. They'd go to school for three months and then I'd fly them home for a month.

Those kids were as young as ten, and their parents sent them away to another country—not too far away, but a different country—for several months at a time. The mail system was unreliable and slow, and telephones were practically non-existent. Witnessing the goodbyes always made me feel sad. Those parents sacrificed all that time that normally would have been spent with their children in order to do their missionary work. That's one of the toughest parts of being a missionary. Bringing the children back home three months later, I shared in the joy. Those were the happy times.

Beth managed the ground office. Her work centered on communicating with me and keeping the records. People would call or write requesting a flight, and she would put them on a calendar. At the end of each month, she handled the billing.

We had an old mimeograph machine at the house, and we would print out the monthly schedules for my flights and get them to all the missionary organizations and commercial outfits working in the country. We were available on a first-call basis to our own missionary personnel and other missionary groups in the country had second call. After that, any empty slots on the schedule were available for commercial use, which helped pay the expenses of the airplane. I flew anywhere from thirty to fifty hours a month for our own missionaries. Any additional passengers I booked helped defray the cost of the flights, which were substantial.

As in every other area of life in Tanzania, the communication system was almost nonexistent. We had our own short-wave radios, but the government had little infrastructure for communications at the major cities. Three cities in Tanzania had control towers at their airports. At all the other strips in the country, you flew in and landed with no information at all. The three major airports also had the only weather information. The government did not supply communication or weather information or traffic control information. This made flying dangerous, and we had to find a way around the problem.

We got permission to use a ham radio to communicate with our people for aviation assistance. A missionary woman, Eva Ennis, operated a ham radio in Kasulu, a city on the western side of Tanzania near the Burundi border. I could talk to her in flight. Beth also had a ham radio. Eva relayed information to me on my airplane radio, she and Beth could talk to each other, and I could talk to both of them. That worked out wonderfully well.

Without those ham radios, if I had gone down for any reason, they would not have known where to look for me. To avoid that eventuality, I checked in with Beth every thirty minutes with a position report. She knew my route, and she could track me. If something had happened, she could have told the government where to look. That was very comforting. Beth monitored the radio constantly when I was flying, and that kept her very busy. I'd usually sign off when I landed: "On the ground, Kasulu," or "On the ground, Mbeya."

Mercy Flights

During the thirteen months Beth and I served in Africa, most of the flying I did was routine—delivering supplies and mail, and carrying visitors to the outlying missions. But I flew three mercy flights for other missionary groups while I was there. Each one touched me deeply and drove home how much the missionary families sacrificed in order to serve.

One Saturday night I received a call from Eva Ennis: "A nurse has fallen and broken her ankle. The medical people told her if she didn't get attention quickly, it would never heal properly. Can you come out and pick her up tomorrow?" The nurse was a nun in the hospital of a Catholic mission outpost about thirty miles from Kasulu. Our policy was not to fly on Sundays, but I really wanted to help out. After discussing it with my mission director, I got the okay. "Yeah, let's go get her," he said.

Kasulu is in northwest Tanzania, near Burundi, about as far as you can get from Dar es Salaam and still be in Tanzania. I couldn't go nonstop that far out and make it back. Our operations manager agreed to accompany me, and after loading three extra jerry cans of fuel, we took off the next morning.

The route to Kasulu took us 650 miles inland over forested hills and low mountains. Though the town is a commercial center for the area, it's quite undeveloped. The red dirt streets are lined with ditches that serve as the water system and wires suspended on rough tree trunks carry electricity to the privileged few. Mud huts give way to sturdier structures with metal roofs in the town center, and the busy, colorful market consists of dozens of tiny sheds bearing what goods are either produced in the area or transported in by airplanes like my own.

As it turned out, getting the nun out of Kasulu was more difficult than we had imagined. She had a splint on her leg, which made it impossible to get her into the airplane without taking the door off. We finally managed to get her into the backseat, and she and her companion made it to Dar es Salaam in relative comfort. If we hadn't been able to fly her out, she would no doubt have been crippled by her injury for life.

Once, while staying over in Mwanza, the second-largest city in Tanzania, with nothing scheduled except to bring a missionary back to Dar es Salaam the next day, I got a call for help. There had been a death in a mission family and they had made arrangements to ship the body back to the US, but the widow wanted to get back, too, and they had no way to get her to Dar es Salaam to catch a commercial flight. It was very easy to add another passenger and a bag or two, but it meant a lot to her. Instead of being left behind, she was able to get back home and bury her husband among consoling family and friends.

The third mercy flight was the saddest of all. I was flying some missionaries from northern Kenya into Mbeya, a town in southwestern Tanzania that sprawls across a narrow valley surrounded by high mountains. A radio operator at the MAF (Missionary Aviation Fellowship) base there called me about an hour out. "We've got a very tragic situation here, and I hope you can help us," he said.

The father of one of the missionary families had been out driving the night before, which was very unusual. The roads were too dangerous in the dark. It was customary to pile tree branches or bushes in the middle of the road a hundred yards from a disabled vehicle as a signal to other drivers. He either missed the branches or they weren't there, and he crashed into a broken down car in his path. The impact killed him instantly.

His wife was pregnant, and they had a little girl about three or four years old. I flew her and her daughter back to Dar es Salaam, and they traveled home from there. These people out there working for the Lord know the risk involved, but that doesn't make these mishaps any less tragic.

The mercy missions, sad as they were, did not make me unhappy. I was just grateful that I could serve the Lord. Being so closely involved with the missions and their families was deeply rewarding for Beth and me. Southern Baptists keep lists such as Open Windows and the Prayer Calendar, which name all their missionaries, their birthdays, and where they are serving. We discovered these early in our married life and prayed for thousands of missionaries every single morning. I still do.

Ascent of Mount Kilimanjaro

Though I spent fifty-seven years in a cockpit, sometimes flying nearly fifty thousand feet above the earth, I experienced a different, uniquely satisfying kind of joy when I climbed to the top of Mount Kilimanjaro and watched the sun rise over Africa from Uhuru Peak. Glaciers and snowfields shimmered blue in first light before the sun bathed them in golden rose. My face stung from the bitter cold, and my lungs ached from the effort of breathing the impossibly thin air at 19,341 feet.

Beth and I had begun the Kilimanjaro trek together at Marangu Gate, 6,250 feet above sea level, four days earlier, on December 27, 1982. At sixty-five years old, we landed squarely on the older side of those who attempt the ascent, but by no means were we the oldest. An eighty-five year old man made the summit not long ago. I wish I had tried it again at that age. I'm pretty sure I would have made it.

Beth and I were traveling with Elizabeth, the daughter of Beth's sister, Ruth. She was teaching English in Eastern Europe for a year and came down to join in the adventure. A group of seven or eight Marines stationed at Dar es Salaam were hiking, too. Coincidentally, they were the same Marines guarding the American ambassador's residence, where six months earlier we had celebrated the Fourth of July.

December 27 is at the tail end of one of the rainy seasons at Mount Kilimanjaro. Temperatures ranged from about fifty degrees at the base to twenty degrees at the summit. On Uhuru Peak, our final destination, the snow was at its deepest, eleven inches on average, more where it accumulated in drifts.

The Marangu route is the only one with huts along the way, where trekkers stop to eat and spend the night. The accommodations are simple dormitories with thin mattresses on the floor. They're just a step above tents, but porters carry all the food and gear, which is quite a luxury. In the mornings, we would see the young men, many of them teenagers, clean up after cooking and serving us breakfast, repack all the gear and lift hundred-pound packs onto their heads. Most astonishing was watching them scramble up the mountain past us as if we were standing still. I considered myself a pretty good athlete, a long-distance runner, including marathons, but these guys were in another league entirely.

The first day of our hike took us through forested slopes, jungle vegetation punctuated by wildflowers and strange succulents that looked like massive century plants. We passed streams and waterfalls and heard the cries of monkeys and birds hidden high up in the canopy. By late afternoon, we arrived at the Mandara Huts and enjoyed a meal cooked by the porters who had raced ahead to prepare it for us. Beth, Elizabeth, and I had climbed over half a vertical mile to 8,934 feet, and we were tired.

The next morning, we got up early, ate breakfast, and hit the trail by 7:30 or 8:00 a.m. It was already chilly, and the higher we got, the lower the temperatures dropped. The second day took us above tree line into what is called the heath and moorland zone. Here the landscape opened almost as wide as the sky, and Kibo, the highest crater and our ultimate destination, came into view.

The climb from the Mandara Huts took us from 8,934 feet to 12,208 feet at day's end. As instructed by our guides, we slowed our pace to give our bodies a chance to acclimatize to the thinning air. By day's end, we made it to the Horombo Huts, a collection of A-frames on the chilly mountainside.

The next morning, the three of us were still feeling fine, and we headed up the mountain to the last camp, the Kibo Huts at 15,466 feet. The terrain changed again, dramatically, and we spent much of the day on what is called The Saddle, a windswept desert that connects Mawenzi and Kibo. At about 16,000 feet, the path became solid snow and ice. Crampons would have been very helpful, but we didn't have them. That year, the rain and snowfall were heavier than usual, and there was more snow than expected. Nowadays, due to climate change, there is much less snow on the mountain. Though it was rough going, we had the intense pleasure of walking all day with the magnificent sight of Kibo, our ultimate destination, in view.

That evening, Beth began to feel the effects of the altitude. She certainly wasn't the only one. The majority don't get far beyond this point. Altitude sickness takes out as many as 77 percent of Kilimanjaro trekkers. Going on is too dangerous unless you are really in a condition to do so.

After a few hours of sleep, we awoke at midnight to make the final ascent of Uhuru Peak. Beth felt too sick to go any higher and decided to stay behind. Wearing flashlights on our heads, our diminishing group walked a trail covered with crusty snow and rocks. Elizabeth stayed with us for about an hour before altitude sickness forced her to turn back. Very soon, I found myself alone with the guide. The other two who made it to the top may have gone ahead. I don't know. The rest didn't make it that far.

Like a marathon, the challenge of the climb is as much mental as it is physical. Some of those who didn't make it to the top, like the Marines, were in great shape, but they at-tacked the mountain instead of taking it on step by step. The Swahili term is pole-pole (easy-easy). I felt lucky to be in good enough shape to get to the top of the world and grateful to the guide who helped me navigate the rough terrain. We reached the summit as the sun rose. I only wished Beth could have been at my side sharing the awe-inspiring moment.

After a short rest, the guide and I walked back down to the Kibo Huts, where Beth and Elizabeth waited. Together we hiked back down to the Horombo Huts, arriving at about five o'clock in the afternoon. I had been walking for seven-teen hours. That sounds worse than it felt. Coming down is easier—hard on the joints but not on the heart because we weren't exercising excessively. After a good night's sleep, we hiked back down to the Maranga Gate, where we'd started five days earlier.

On the first day of the trek, one of the Marines Elizabeth befriended said, "I saw your aunt and uncle, and my, they're quite elderly, aren't they?" We had the last laugh, though. Only one of the seven Marines made it to the top!

LAST FLIGHT

"One day a pilot is going to walk out to his airplane knowing it's going to be his last flight, or one day he's going to walk out to his airplane not knowing it's going to be his last flight."
— Anonymous

I wanted to know.

In Tanzania, I flew a Cessna 210, a beautiful high-wing six-passenger retractable-gear airplane. It was fast and efficient, and I loved flying it. When I came back to the US in 1983, I found two people who shared ownership of a Cessna 210. They were looking to replace a third partner who wanted out, and I bought his interest.

I could take the plane and fly anytime I wanted to as long as none of the other partners reserved it. I often flew locally, over north Texas, for an hour or two or three. Sometimes Beth accompanied me on these outings. Occasionally we checked out the plane for two or three days and flew to Angel Fire in the New Mexico mountains, where we owned a condominium.

Once, when two of our granddaughters were quite young, we flew them to Washington, D.C. These were wonderful trips, and I thoroughly enjoyed flying just for the pleasure of it.

Nevertheless, by the time I hit my seventies, some of the thrill had gone out of piloting a plane. Keeping my qualification to fly on instruments had become a big part of the problem. I always loved flying on instruments. It never bothered me a bit unless there was a thunderstorm involved or icing. Flying is so much more than operating controls. There's an old saying: "Never let your airplane take you somewhere your brain didn't get to five minutes earlier." You've got to be looking and planning ahead. Now they call that multitasking, and, as I get older, I find that is becoming more difficult.

When you're flying in the clouds, you cannot instinctively know which way is up or down. It's impossible. If you're upside down, the centrifugal force overcomes gravity to the point where your brain thinks down is up. Consequently, there are at least three gauges that you must observe. You can't do it continuously, but you must check them every few seconds to be sure you're doing things right. Total focus on your various tasks is essential.

Now imagine you're in an instrument situation, but you're not observing your instruments. When you finally get around to checking, you notice a loss of altitude. Normally, the proper response is to pull back on the control column. But if the plane is in a turn, this only tightens up the turn, usually allowing the bank to increase and the nose to drop. That increases the loss of altitude. At this point, the appropriate response is to level the wings to stop the turn and then regain the lost altitude. However, if only backpressure on the control column is used, the nose drops further, and the airspeed increases rapidly to and beyond the red line (the maximum airspeed allowed). Remember, this is all happening in a matter of seconds. Your reaction time has to be instantaneous.

Once you're at redline, you're in the graveyard (or death) spiral. If you don't correct it, you'll never realize you're not right-side up, because gravity is where the seat of your pants tells you it is, and you can be way off.

The death spiral is the most severe consequence of failing to watch your instruments, but there are plenty of other negative outcomes. When you're flying on instruments, you're rotating your attention between three or four different gauges. At the same time, you're constantly thinking: *Where am I going? What's the weather up ahead? How much fuel do I have? Do I have enough to get there and go to an alternate if the weather is bad?* All of this is going through your head the whole time you're flying. If you're flying straight and level, that's fine, but if you're going someplace without realizing what the weather might be when you get there, or how much fuel you're going to have when you get there, you're not flying the airplane.

Conditions can change rapidly during any flight. You always have to be ready to fly on instruments, and pilots have to remain current to fly under instrument conditions. When you're in a cloud and can't see where you are, you're on instrument flight rules. To fly under instrument flight rules conditions you have to be qualified. You have to have flown under instruments for six hours in the last six months. As I got older, that became difficult. I could have substituted flying in a simulator, but to rent a simulator costs money. I could have also had someone fly in the airplane with me. They would have put a hood over my head to prevent me from seeing. That didn't seem very appealing to me either.

In addition to flying under instruments, pilots have to keep their manuals up to date in order to fly. The manuals delineate how to fly on instruments, where to fly on instruments, and instrument approach procedures for every airport where you intend to land.

Manual revisions come out at least two or three times a

month, and they might be ten or twenty pages long. Regulations regarding how to fly, when to fly, and where to fly change all the time. So do the federal air regulations. The revised pages have to be replaced in the flight manual you carry in the airplane at all times. Keeping up with all those revisions got to be a chore for me. I began to question if flying was still worth all this effort.

I also had to face the very real fact that I was slowing down and aviation was speeding up. I still felt in full control of the airplane and confident I could effectively, efficiently, and safely fly under all conditions. But I thought, *Hey, it's not going to be much longer now. I might as well hang it up while I'm still enjoying it and before I have an accident.*

I spent more than fifty-seven years piloting airplanes, using my brain to full capacity. I didn't have the kind of job you can do without giving it too much thought. After I retired from Braniff, I continued flying regularly with JAARS, and I enjoyed flying that Cessna 210 with Beth and my family. That was the last airplane I owned.

My first and last passenger accompanied me on my final flight. Beth and I flew over North Texas for the last time on a clear, beautiful day in 1996. Then I put my interest up for sale.

When I finally gave up flying at age seventy-nine, my life changed dramatically. I miss it, but it's like anything else. Time moves on. We have to adapt.

THE RUNNING
MAN

Starting at age twenty-two, when I flew solo for the first time, nothing else equaled the thrill I experienced in the air. I loved surveying the breadth of God's creation below, flying free among the clouds, and stretching and challenging my brain's capacity to focus on the myriad details involved in piloting an airplane. I would have missed flying desperately if I had not had another activity that pushed my body and mind to its limits. By the time I gave up flying at age seventy-nine, I had been running competitively for nearly thirty years. And I was good at it.

In 1968, after racing through Dr. Cooper's first book, *Aerobics*, I literally hit the ground running. I laced up my Keds sneakers and progressed fairly quickly to daily three-or-four mile runs. It didn't occur to me to take it a little easier. I'm just not built that way. And I'd never heard of doing any kind of stretching exercises. I just took off in those terrible sneakers on hard pavement and never looked back. I didn't slow down until a couple of years later, when I developed Achilles tendinitis in both legs. If you've ever had it, you know that will talk to you.

Dr. Cooper to the Rescue

Dr. Cooper retired from the Air Force and moved to Dallas in 1970, where he opened the Cooper Clinic at Preston Center. By then he had already earned renown for using his aerobics training methods with the Brazilian soccer team, which went on to win the World Cup.

I had met Dr. Cooper the year before, when he came to Dallas to give a talk, so I called him up and made an appointment. He examined me, and gave me three things to treat the tendonitis: He showed me how to stretch properly. He said I should run on grass for a while, and he told me to drop back to one-mile runs, then work back up gradually to five kilometers. Those three simple changes cured me and reinforced my faith in Dr. Cooper. In 1972, he agreed to do my annual physical. I've been back every year since, and, in 2016, I'll have my forty-fourth annual physical with him.

With the tremendous success of Dr. Cooper's book on physical fitness, the Cooper Clinic became world famous. In 1971 they bought a property in North Dallas and created a beautiful campus that includes state-of-the-art workout facilities, a research and education center, and a preventive medicine clinic, where staff physicians give thousands of physicals a year, inspiring their patients to become or stay physically active.

Numerous scientific studies from around the world add to the research that is conducted at the Cooper Clinic, all of them published and peer reviewed. They prove conclusively that exercise promotes good health and longevity. One such paper published in 2012, *Leisure Time Physical Activity of Moderate to Vigorous Intensity and Mortality: A Large Pooled Cohort Analysis* (http://dx.doi.org/10.1371/journal.pmed.1001335), draws on six major studies involving more than 650,000 people followed for over ten years. These studies found that, on average, exercising at the recommended minimum level added 3.4 years to participants' life spans after age forty, and vigorous exercise doubles that number. I calculate that my training and racing have added 6.8 years to my life. That's a pretty good bargain.

Cooperisms

- Physical fitness is a journey, not a destination.
- If you cannot find time to exercise now, you had better find time to be sick.
- Walk your dog twice a day whether you have a dog or not.
- Age fast, age slow, it's up to you.
- You don't wear out, you rust out.
- It is cheaper and more efficient to maintain good health than to regain it.

Stress Test for President Bush

Dr. Cooper treats many high-profile patients. Among them is George W. Bush, who began seeing him when he lived in Dallas. This is the story Dr. Cooper told me about treating President Bush. He had been giving Bush his annual physical for many years, and when he became president in 2001, he wanted to continue that tradition.

During his first year in office, he contacted Dr. Cooper and asked him to fly to Washington, D.C., to give him his annual physical at the Bethesda Naval Hospital. The chief of cardiology was present, of course, and he asked Dr. Cooper what kind of physical he intended to conduct with the president.

Dr. Cooper described the type of physical he had done for Bush in the past and told him which lab tests he wanted. So far so good. Then he told the cardiologist about the treadmill stress test to exhaustion, and the guy went into orbit.

"You're going to kill the president," he said.

Dr. Cooper, in his customary soft-pedal way retorted, "Well, sir, we have given over one hundred thousand physicals at the Cooper Clinic. We're currently giving over eight thousand a year, and we haven't lost anyone yet."

Dr. Cooper gave Bush his physical, and as we all know, Bush survived. I never had a moment of doubt about Dr. Cooper's practices. In my mind, he's done more for the health of our country than anyone, and I'm very pleased that he continues to give me his personal attention for my annual physical and throughout the year.

The Cooper Clinic Physical

When you go in for a physical at the Cooper Clinic, you do your treadmill stress test and all your lab work first thing in the morning. By noon or one o'clock, all the labs are completed and the results of your stress test are in. Then the doctor sits down with you and discusses the whole picture of your physical fitness and any problems that have been detected. Knowing how much the clinic has done for me, I've sent a lot of people over there. I just wish everyone could have access to such good preventive medicine.

In 1992, my trip to the Cooper Clinic for an annual physical literally saved my life. I was on the treadmill for my stress test when Dr. Cooper intervened. He stopped the machine and helped me down. "You've got a problem," he said.

The stress test indicated blockages, and further testing at

Baylor confirmed Dr. Cooper's diagnosis. Six of my arteries were 80 to 95 percent blocked.

On January 5, 1993, I had bypass surgery on all six blockages. The operation was a complete success, but I subsequently developed an infection in my knee where they had removed a section of a vein to use in the surgery. That hiccup didn't slow my recovery too badly, and in six weeks I was back on the track.

A few years later, a full body scan indicated all six of the native arteries were fully blocked and all six bypasses were wide open. Without the surgery, I would have been dead.

That surgery was the most dramatic outcome of any of my annual physicals at Cooper, though they are always very complete, thorough, exhaustive examinations. After I have my labs and stress test, Dr. Cooper usually spends at least thirty minutes to an hour with me, which I think is very kind and pretty unusual in this hurry-up day and age.

During my physical at age eighty or so, Dr. Cooper and I had the customary discussion about my health. "How do you feel about your situation?" he said.

"Well I think I'm doing pretty good, except maybe I'm having a little trouble with my short-term memory," I said.

His eyebrows shot up.

I paused to let that sink in before I said, "And another thing, I may be having trouble with my short-term memory."

He didn't laugh. He's not really a laugh-out-loud type. But he smiled.

The Dallas Running Club

I joined the Cross Country Club of Dallas, now called the Dallas Running Club, in 1969, when I first started running. Founded in 1969 by Tal Morrison, a famous runner in the Dallas area, the club sponsored races on the first Saturday of the month, and I competed for many years. Their minimum distance is a mile, and their competitions vary each month. They also sponsor the annual Dallas Marathon, formerly the White Rock Marathon.

I ran the White Rock Marathon for the first time when I was fifty-six or fifty-seven years old. It's just impossible to anticipate your first marathon no matter how much or how hard you train. A lot of people hit the wall because they aren't prepared for the punishment a body takes under those circumstances. There's a saying that the length of the marathon is 26.2 miles, but the halfway point is twenty miles. The last six miles are as hard as the first twenty.

It's generally recommended to train for a marathon by running sixteen, then eighteen, then twenty miles before tackling twenty-six. A good training program calls for running at least twenty-five or thirty miles a week with several races of that length spaced a week apart. That was how I trained for my first marathon, and I still crashed at the twenty-three mile mark. The drive to finish didn't diminish, but I could only walk a few hundred yards, then take a few running steps before slowing down to walking again. I could not reach the finish line any other way. Dr. Cooper saw me cross the finish line of my first marathon. I think he was proud of me. I certainly felt I'd accomplished something important.

Someone once described how he felt after climbing Mount Rainier, saying that when he got down, he hurt all over worse than anyplace else. Funny as that sounds, that's exactly how it was for me. Every cell in my body was totally exhausted. Surprisingly, I was not sore the next day. I didn't run for two or three days, but after that short break, I got right back into it.

The next marathon was in Tulsa about a year later, and it was the worst race I've ever run anywhere, anytime. The weather was terrible. The temperature was about thirty-eight degrees. There was a light drizzle, and a fifteen- to twenty-mile-an-hour northwest wind. It was brutal, but I finished. Beth wrapped me in a blanket at the finish. She took good care of me.

I competed in five marathons. The White Rock Marathon was my last. I was seventy-five years old, and I beat a twenty-year-old by thirty minutes. My time was three hours, thirty-nine minutes, and some seconds.

"It's all in the pacing," I told that young man before the race, but he didn't listen to me.

He was the son of a good friend, and this was his first marathon. I asked him about his training schedule. It wasn't impressive, as I recall.

"I've run four marathons," I said, "and I think I'm fairly well qualified to advise you about how to run your first marathon. Considering the training you've done, I would recommend you start out at about the same pace I plan to run the whole thing. If you want to run with me, that's fine, or you can just maintain that pace on your own."

I don't remember how fast my pace was, but it was pretty slow. "Run that for at least the first two or three hours. If you're feeling good at that point, you might try increasing your pace a little bit, but only if you think you have enough reserves to go the remaining distance."

Well, he stayed with me for the first five or six miles, and then he just couldn't stand it anymore. He took off running faster.

I passed him at the twenty-mile mark. He was walking!

That gave me a fair amount of pleasure, and passing him might have had something to do with how well I did. I finished that race in my best time ever. It was gratifying to be able to achieve that, because not many people my age were doing nearly that well. I don't know why I never ran another marathon. I guess I was so happy about my time, I decided five marathons were enough.

I remained active in the Dallas Running Club until I was eighty years old, participating in their races and taking home awards. I had a great friend in the club named Dick Granger. He was just about the same age, and a strong competitor. In the early years, I never could beat him, but as we both got older, he slowed down considerably. When we hit age eighty, he had to quit running altogether. I kept at it for a while, but I could not run the longer distances.

Once Dick quit, there was nobody my age to compete with, and that's no fun. For me, running is a competitive sport. If I'm not reaching for the top, aiming to be the best, I'm not interested.

TRAINING OUTSIDE THE BOX

One of the biggest challenges of racing at my age is avoiding injuries and keeping my body in condition. Younger competitors have trainers for that, but I never found a trainer who works with older runners. There are only a few runners my age who have gone through similar life experiences and have reached the point of declining physical fitness that naturally comes with aging. But we don't communicate between meets and don't share tips on how we approach training. I read a book by the Canadian runner Earl Fee and gleaned some good information from him, but he's about ten years younger than I am, and that makes a difference.

The upshot is, I have lost all faith in trying to find anybody, coach or participant, to consult with about the best methods of training and running.

I do trust Dr. Cooper's advice on staying in shape, but even he does not know what my body's limits are or how I can work around them. Once again, I am flying outside the box, creating new rules, taking calculated risks.

About fifteen years ago, Dr. Cooper asked me how far I was running.

"I run three miles a day and ten miles around the lake on Saturdays," I said.

"At your age, I think that's too much," he said. "I'm going to limit you to five miles at a time from now on."

"Thank you, thank you, thank you!" Believe me, I was ready to hear that I didn't need to run ten miles to stay proficient.

When it comes to taking care of my knees, I listen to Dr. Howard Moore, my orthopedist. He's a former neighbor, and he invited me to come into his office for a physical about five years ago, when I was ninety-three. After looking at the X-rays of my knees, he said "I hope my knees are in as good a shape as yours when I get to be your age. But I would advise you to cut your running back a little bit and do some of your aerobic work on a treadmill or an elliptical machine. Do a slow build-up to boost endurance rather than speed."

Dr. Cooper and Dr. Moore know what they're talking about, and I respect their judgment. For the most part, I'll do what they suggest, but I know my body and its limits better than anyone. Consequently, I make my own rules. I've had to get creative and come up with my own approach, adapting my version of Earl Fee's schedule of interval training to stay physically fit and to get into top condition for a meet.

THE ROGERS
REGIMEN

Rules for Training at Age Ninety and Beyond

1. I begin with stretching, and then I put in about thirty minutes on the elliptical. That's about a mile and a half, and it gets me started without any pounding on my feet. Pounding on your feet strengthens your bones, so it's good for you as long as it's not excessive. I probably ought to be doing a little boxing or punching a bag to strengthen my arm bones, but as I said, I make my own rules.

2. After the treadmill or elliptical, I get on the track. The weather in Dallas is frequently too hot or too cold or too rainy, so I just stay indoors. The Cooper Center has a nice track with a rubberized surface that makes it softer than most. And it's measured off in lengths that you can use to measure your distance and your time. If I'm training for a race, I run a certain

distance and check my time daily. That way I can keep tabs on my progress.

3. I usually run about a mile at a slow speed for my warm-up. I've run about two and a half miles before I get serious about it. Then I run some speed work—if you can count any running at the age of ninety-eight as speedy. The proper term for this part of the workout is *interval training*. There are a number of protocols you can follow, but I devised my own. Earl Fee recommends running fast for a minute and then two minutes slow or something like that. I can't do that.

4. This is the interval training I devised for myself: After I've warmed up and run a mile or more, I rest a while to let my pulse rate go down. Then I run 100 meters as fast as I can. After that sprint, I walk 100 or 200 meters to cool down and let my heart recover a little bit more. Then I run another hundred meters all out. I follow with another cooldown and rest. I may or may not do a third sprint, depending on how I feel. I usually don't run more than three or four miles altogether, and during the rest periods, I do more stretching.

5. Cooling down is critical. Jim Fixx, the famous runner who wrote *The Complete Book of Running*, died of a heart attack after a training run. The speculation is that he did not cool down. He may have had a heart problem of some kind, but, in any case, he broke a cardinal rule. It is recommended to maintain some level of activity until your heart rate is below one hundred. The theory is, when you are exercising vigorously, your heart is pumping large amounts of blood, and your muscles are pumping that blood back to your heart. The leg muscles are referred to as the second heart, because the muscle contractions of your legs act as a pump that returns the venous blood back to the heart. There it is renewed with oxygen and food supply that is distributed back into the arterial

system. If you stop running or exercising abruptly, these muscles are not pumping the blood back to the heart fast enough to keep up with the demand. The heart is still racing. It takes time to slow down. The cool-down period ensures the needed blood supply for the heart.

I wear a chest strap equipped with a radio transmitter that signals a watch-size armband that continuously displays my heart rate. My cardiologists tell me it's very important to watch that. Unless I'm in a race and don't want the encumbrance slowing me down, I always wear that device when I run.

6. After the final cooldown and recovery period, I lift weights for thirty to forty minutes. Assuming the running is taking care of leg strengthening, I concentrate on the upper body and arms. I do five strengthening exercises on my upper torso and arms. That's very important for athletes and non-athletes alike. If you need to hold onto a railing going down a stairway, you need some arm strength. If you start to fall and your arm is not strong enough to hold you, you'll plunge down the steps. That's training for everyday life.

If I'm not training for a race, this is the extent of my workout. I do it faithfully, three times a week. I rarely suffer any injury or ill health, so I would say, give it try. It works for me.

Preparing for a Meet

It's one thing to maintain good physical fitness and quite another to train for a race. I think the consensus is that the best peak physical fitness you can attain is done by a gradual increase in speed and distance, and in the final weeks before a meet, you adopt a schedule of running fast and then running slowly, then running fast and running slowly, over and over.

You cannot maintain your maximum fitness for more than a month or so. Something will break down if you're training at peak levels for an extended period of time. That's the theory that all the well-known coaches and athletes subscribe to in one form or another.

I train at a basic level three times a week to maintain my strength and aerobic capacity. A month or two before a meet, I begin building up to a peak. The aim is to reach a peak ten to fourteen days before the event. I coast down after that peak and do less and less running as the meet date approaches. That way, I am not exhausted when the time comes to run all out.

I may not have a professional trainer, but I have developed a regimen that enabled me to set fifteen world records. Now I'm turning my attention to developing a training program with assistance from Elizabeth Murphy, an assistant throwing coach at Southern Methodist University in Dallas. She will help me prepare to compete in some field events along with the track competitions in 2018, when I move into the one-hundred-year-old-and-above bracket. Stay tuned!

RECORD
BREAKER

After I left the Dallas Running Club, I continued running, first at Baylor Landry and later at the Cooper Campus. Then, when I was approaching the age of ninety, I thought I'd look into competing nationally. I knew that USA Track & Field kept records by five-year brackets, so I looked up the ninety- to ninety-four-year-old bracket. *Hey*, I thought, *I can do that*.

I figured I'd compete well in the 1-mile and the 800-meter. So I started training. I engaged a trainer at Baylor Landry and worked with him for two or three months. He gave me some very good pointers about pacing and striding and breathing and everything that would help me increase my speed and endurance. I was already breathing well, but I learned how to breathe effectively with my strides. He cautioned me to always try to run a straight line because straying from that takes energy, and he taught me to pace myself. On the longer runs, he told me to start out slow, or I'd end up exhausted before the finish line. Much of his training was a refinement of what I already knew, but it was very helpful.

My first race outside of Dallas was the National Championship Indoor Meet in Boston, March 22, 2008. Beth planned to accompany me, and we purchased our airline tickets months in advance.

Two weeks before the race, my world crashed.

Beth died on March 8. I lost my companion, my partner in every area of my life, the most important person in the world to me.

Until ten days before her death, she had been just fine, still doing her daily walks, active as ever. Then a triple whammy hit her: pneumonia, kidney failure, and a blood infection. We had a good day together on the Thursday before she died, and I thought she might recover. But on Friday she took a turn for the worse, and on Saturday she fell into a coma. She passed away that night.

We had been together for nearly seventy years, married sixty-four years, nine months, and five days. Losing her meant losing my own life, or so it seemed. In truth, it only felt that way, and as the reality of her passing sank in, I knew I could not honor her memory or my Lord by giving up on life. I had to go on without her.

I talked with my children about following through with the competition in Boston. They all agreed their mom would have wanted me to go ahead and run. Accompanied by my daughter, Susan, my son Rick, and my son Bill and his wife Melanie I went to Boston deep in grief, not at all confident that I was in any shape to compete, much less win. My first race was the 800-meter. I ran it in 4:19.97 and broke the world record. The next day I ran the 1-mile in 9:56.58, which broke the record by a minute and a half. I slaughtered it! I have to think Beth was there with me. I know God was. How else could I have found the will to triumph amid my deepest despair?

After that first meet, there were no real records I could break in my age bracket. At least, I didn't think so. Back in Dallas, I kept running, and periodically, I attended meets in the US and Canada. It's always fun to take part in these competitions. They aren't that well attended, but the couple hundred spectators that show up are an enthusiastic cheering squad for the participants, which number somewhere between 1,000 and 1,200.

Though I enjoy the experience, traveling to meets is expensive and time consuming. Consequently, I am very selective. I don't participate in regional meets at all, only national championship meets, usually one indoor and one outdoor a year. Unlike many of the regional competitions, the nationals have very accurate timing equipment and very good people staffing them. Their times are always acceptable to the world organization that keeps track of the world records. If you set a record in the US, it is almost inevitably accepted as a world record.

Sidelined

I was thoroughly enjoying running and traveling to the national meets, and then, on March 8, 2011, the third anniversary of Beth's death, I had a major stroke. It was eight or nine o'clock at night. Bill and his wife, Melanie, who had joined me for dinner, had just left, and I was sitting at my dining room table, replenishing my daily vitamins and medications in their plastic compartments.

Without any notice, my left arm started to tingle. At first it was very subtle, just a little bit of a tingle. But it grew more and more pronounced. It will pass, I thought, just like lots of other odd feelings that come and go. I ignored it for a while, but it continued to spread and the tingling intensified.

I remembered the self-tests for determining if you have had a stroke, and I stood up. A stroke is the result of a blockage or rupture of an artery. It affects only one side of the brain. If the ruptured artery is in the right side of the brain, your left side is affected in some way and vice versa. The first test is to stand there and see if your feet work equally well, see if your arms work equally well, and see if your eyes see equally well and if you can flick them left and right. Next, try to talk. If you're paralyzed on one vocal cord, you can't talk. I ran through all the tests, and everything seemed perfectly normal.

I sat back down and tried to ignore the strange sensations, but they just kept getting worse. In just a few minutes, the tingling ran from my wrist to my elbow. Despite the fact that I was not experiencing the major symptoms of a stroke, I knew something was very wrong.

I called 911, took an aspirin, and headed across the den to my front door.

As I walked, my left foot started dragging. That's when I knew for sure. I went out and sat down on the front step to wait for the ambulance. Five minutes later a fire truck arrived.

"The ambulance has to come from a little bit further, but they'll be here shortly," the fire-fighters said.

The ambulance got there another five minutes later, and the EMTs sat down with me and asked me a bunch of questions. *Why don't you take me to the emergency room?* I thought. "I'm having a stroke, and I know I'm having a stroke, so just take me to the hospital."

I didn't say any of that out loud. I figured they knew what they were doing. They kept asking me what my symptoms were and how I felt, and I started growing quite impatient. *Let's get on with it,* I thought.

When they finally put me in the ambulance, they told me they had to make sure I was experiencing what I said I was experiencing because they have people call in who just want a free ride downtown. Can you imagine?

That was the roughest ride I've ever experienced. That ambulance had no springs whatsoever, and every little bump was magnified. I wanted to complain about it, but I was more concerned about my condition, which was deteriorating fast. Halfway to the hospital, my left foot and hand were totally paralyzed. I could not move a finger or a toe or even move my wrist or my foot. I was absolutely, totally paralyzed and very, very anxious.

We arrived at the Baylor Emergency Room within thirty minutes, which is well within the two-hour limit for administering a clot buster. In no time at all, an IV dripped the clot-busting medication into my arm. I watched that drip from the pint-size container, and by the time it was half empty, feeling began to return in my hand. I was able to move it.

A few minutes later, after all the medicine had been administered, my hand and foot were paralyzed again. That was discouraging. Nothing changed by the next morning, when two nurses helped me stand. My right foot bore all the weight. *Am I ever going to walk again,* I wondered, *much less run?*

I transferred to the rehabilitation unit a couple days later and met with the head honcho. "I want you to give me the most rigorous rehab program you can give me," I said.

"We'll do that."

And they did. I began to improve within a day or two, and gradually the feeling came back. By the end of a week, I had full use of my left hand and foot, though they were considerably weakened. Gradually my fears that I would never run again abated, and I felt optimistic.

Not long after my return home, I woke up one morning to that same tingling feeling in my left forefinger and my left thumb. I was afraid I'd had another stroke, so I saw a neurologist, who had me undergo another MRI. There was no evidence of a stroke. Those fingers still tingle when I move them, and when I'm motionless, they're numb. I have difficulty buttoning my collar button and sometimes my sleeve button, especially if the buttons are small. Apparently this is the one minor dysfunction that will never go away. Considering other possible outcomes, I feel blessed. God watches over me. How else to explain that I came back from complete immobility to running races and breaking world records?

Back in the Race

At age ninety-five, I traveled to Landover, Maryland, for the National Indoor Championship, and that's when the door blew wide open. I set five world records at that meet: the 400 meters, the 3,000 meters, the 800 meters, the 200 meters, and the one mile. That same year, I went to the Outdoor National Championship and set the outdoor record in 400 meters. That brought my world records up to eight.

There isn't much competition when you get to be my age, and that makes it a little harder to do your best, but I have to think I was running at peak performance that year. When I competed in the ninety to ninety-four age bracket, there were no more than one or two other runners. There may have been one or two when I got into the ninety-five to ninety-nine age bracket. It's difficult to remember exactly how many runners were in my bracket, because sometimes they would combine heats. I would run in the ninety to ninety-four group, but they'd combine that with the eighty-five to ninety. Although I was sharing the track with runners outside my bracket, the record times were kept only in my age group. There'd be three or four or five younger runners and me. Sometimes I beat one or two runners five years younger than I.

Running on the outdoor track at the Landover meet may have had something to do with how well I did. There's a difference in the length of the tracks and the straightaways at indoor and outdoor competitions, and that changes how you run the race. The outdoor tracks are 400meters around with a

100-meter straightaway. The straightaway is where you really hit it. I can go all out for about a hundred meters, and then I tire. Anything over a hundred meters, I have to slow down in order to finish competitively.

The indoor tracks are 200 meters around, and they have a 60-meter straightaway. The 200-meter is one lap around the indoor track, the 400-meter is two laps, and the 800-meter is four laps. Most records set are slower on indoor tracks. I imagine that the shorter straightaway has something to do with that. There are more turns on an indoor track, and every one slows you down.

Some of my Christian friends have asked me if I ever pray when I'm running, and the answer is no. I've tried it, and my mind just drifts away from the task at hand. When I'm racing, I have to concentrate on my running, my breathing, my footsteps, and my pace. It's a real challenge of focus, and I'm good at it. My training as a pilot was excellent preparation. The ability to multitask, paying attention to a bank of instruments and everything else going on around you, is ideal training for the mental aspect of running. I devote all of my mind and body and spirit to winning the race.

INDIVIDUAL WORLD RECORDS

2008
Boston, Massachusetts

800 meters	04:19.997
1 mile	09:56.580

2013
Landover, Maryland

60 meters	14.82
200 meters	57.88
400 meters	02:24.510
800 meters	06:53.840
1 mile	14:39.910

3,000 meters   30:19.330

(All of the 2013 times were listed as world records at the time; however, only five of them were confirmed.)

* * *

In March 2015, I competed in Winston-Salem, North Carolina, at a new indoor track there. I ran a few individual races just for the fun of it, and then I joined my team and competed in the relays. We managed to get four men in the ninety to ninety-nine age group. (In the relays, the brackets are in ten-year increments.) We ran the 4 by 200 meters, the 4 by 400 meters, and the 4 by 800 meters. That means four runners, four laps. A 4 by 200, for example, is four people running 200 meters each. Each runner runs a lap and must hand off the baton to the next runner within a 10-meter passing zone.

We set world records in relay for each one of those races. Essentially the same team assembled the previous August, also in Winston-Salem at an outdoor meet, and we ran the same races, setting three world records.

I would like to think I was the best one on the team but I really wasn't. I was pretty average. My distance running has suffered greatly. I still have a little bit of speed up to 100 meters, but beyond that I've slowed down a lot. Each of us on that team is in much the same shape. We're getting old, but at least we're out there running.

RELAY WORLD RECORDS

2014
Outdoor Track, Winston-Salem, North Carolina
4X100
02:22.370
Champion Goldy
Orville Rogers

Roy Englert
Charles Ross

4X400
12:41.690
Orville Rogers
Charles Boyle
Roy Englert
Charles Ross

4X800
28:17
Orville Rogers
Charles Boyle
Roy Englert
Charles Ross

2015
Indoor Track, Winston-Salem, North Carolina
4X200
05:40.820
Orville Rogers
Charles Ross
Roy Englert
Charles Boyle

4X400
12:54.810
Orville Rogers
Charles Ross
Dixon Hemphill
Roy Englert

4X800
29:47.680
Orville Rogers
Charles Ross

Roy Englert
Dixon Hemphill

* * *

In 2013, when I set five world records in Landover, Maryland, fifteen members of my family and my old friend from JAARS, Bernie May, were there to cheer me on. During every race, they held up a big banner about two feet high and fifteen feet long that said "Run, Orville, Run." They got the whole spectator section cheering for me. That's quite a thrill, and it may very well have been a factor in my success that day and every time I race. Though I'm deeply focused on what I'm doing, I can hear them cheering for me, and it pushes me on.

* * *

In March 2016, I competed in the National Indoor Championship in Albuquerque, New Mexico. Once again, I had my cheering squad. My sons, Bill and Rick, attended, as well as my grandson, Steven. Paul Wilson from Curtis's squadron in Vietnam came to watch me run both days. On Friday night, I hosted a dinner for Sari Aviv and the rest of the CBS television crew who were filming the races for a *CBS Sunday Morning* report on nonagenarian athletes that aired on August 7, 2016. My friend and fellow racer Dixon Hemphill and I were featured prominently in the broadcast. It was an exciting time.

I decided to run some of the shorter events just for the experience of it. There are no available world records that I can make, but it's fun to be a part of the group. I think it helps to keep the competitive spirit going. I have no records to set for two more years, when I reach the age of one hundred, but I'm not just going to sit back and relax, waiting until the last minute to train for those races. Setting records isn't everything. I always enjoy participating in the championship meets for the simple pleasure of getting together with the runners and field-event people I've known for years.

I suppose the CBS filming had something to do with my desire to do well at this meet, though I always want to do my best. There were some challenges. Albuquerque is at 5,500 feet, which is a mile higher than Dallas. Flying in the day before did not give me any time to acclimate to the altitude. My system was already a bit compromised after a respiratory illness that laid me low in late winter. I hadn't felt strong enough or well enough to train until about two weeks before the meet. Though I couldn't enter the race at peak condition, I was able to go into the competition at my normal fitness level.

For me, the most difficult race was the 1,500 meters. The track at Cooper is measured in yards and miles, so to prepare I timed myself running a mile, then subtracted about a minute from my time. That wasn't exact, but 1,500 meters is 93 percent of a mile, and one minute was about 93 percent of the time it took me to run a mile. That shows you how professional my training program is. But I work with what I've got.

I had expected to run the 1,500-meter in seventeen minutes. To my surprise, I beat that time by twenty-seven seconds. I did better than expected in all my races at Albuquerque, partly, I think, because I had been running on a circular track at the Cooper Clinic, which slows you down a little bit. I really worked hard on the 200-meter, thinking I might be able to do it in 1:20. Instead, thanks to the longer straightaway on the track in Albuquerque, I ran faster and did it in 1:07. I ran a little bit over the seventeen seconds I expected to do in the 60-meter, but that's okay.

It was fun to compete with my old friend Dixon, who was ninety-three at the time. I stayed up with him after the first lap of the 1,500-meter, but after that he stayed ahead of me. I never could catch him. I did beat him in the 60- and 200-meter. That was some consolation.

I felt wonderful during all the races, and I paced myself well. That's important. If you start out too fast, you hit the wall. And at my age, that wall is closer and closer. It takes longer to recover, too. After the euphoria wore off, it took about a week to get back to feeling normal.

Every meet inspires me to continue competing vigorously as a runner. The top distance that I've run is 3,000 meters, and I will compete in that when the time comes, if I'm able. I'll run the shorter events as well.

In addition to track, there are always field events at these meets, and there are few records in the one-hundred-year-old-and-above bracket. I'd like to compete in jumping or pole vaulting or discus throwing if I make it to one hundred. It would be fun to see how far I could throw a discus or a shot put or see how well I could jump at that age. If I start training now, I'll be ready to compete in two years.

* * *

Since I picked up Ken Cooper's *Aerobics* that fateful day in 1968, running has continuously enhanced my quality of life. Thanks to running, I am healthy and vigorous long past the time when others are suffering and in decline. I have goals to work toward, and that is energizing. Competing in the national championships, I have forged lasting friendships. I have a regimen that keeps my body fit and helps ward off the stresses of daily life. I could go on and on about the benefits of my chosen sport, but I want to give credit where credit is due.

I would have none of this but for the fact that God gave me this strong body built for running. In gratitude and as a believer, I have lived by the Word of God: "[D]o you not know that your body is a temple of the Holy Spirit within you, whom you have from God? You are not your own, for you were bought with a price. So glorify God in your body" (1 Corinthians 6:19–20, brackets mine).

THE GIFT OF GIVING

I have spent a lifetime in service to my Lord, and the experiences have enriched my spirit immeasurably. As a Christian, I have also had a lifelong commitment to giving financially. Though I did not expect earthly rewards for my tithing, I received them beyond my wildest dreams.

My earnings from the military and Braniff Airlines totaled $1,550,000. Yet Beth and I gave away over $34,000,000, and that number has continued to rise since her passing. I believe the only way we could have accumulated so much wealth was by giving it away. God knew we would give back as much as we possibly could, and he helped us grow and grow in abundance. God was, and continues to be, involved in every aspect of my life, including my finances.

Jesus said, "Thus, when you give to the needy, sound no trumpet before you, as the hypocrites do in the synagogues and in the streets, that they may be praised by others. Truly, I say to you, they have received their reward" (Matthew 6: 2-4). In other words, when you give to impress others instead of to do God's will, your reward is limited to earthly things. God will not reward you.

This admonishment makes me reluctant to talk too much about my financial success or my tithing. In all the years I have given time, energy, and money to help spread God's Word, I have rarely spoken about it. But I think it's important to talk about our giving now in order to encourage others. My story illustrates the very real connection between giving and abundance. "You are the light of the world," Jesus said. "A city set on a hill cannot be hidden. Nor do people light a lamp and put it under a basket, but on a stand, and it gives light to all in the house. In the same way, let your light shine before others, so that they may see your good works and give glory to your Father who is in heaven" (Matthew 5:14–16). I think that verse is justification for making our giving known. I think God would approve.

* * *

At the beginning of this story, I talked about my mother's brothers, Bill and Ralph Johnston, who were very successful in the oil and gas business. After my father left us, Uncle Bill was especially helpful to us. He always made sure we had enough money to get by. To our great surprise, when he died in 1954, he left my mother, my sister, and me a one twenty-fourth interest in his estate. This included stocks and bonds, oil and gas properties, and ranchland. Altogether, our share was worth a little less than $100,000.

My uncle's estate was settled in 1956, two years after his death. We sold our stake in the ranches, and I got into the oil and gas business. My share from my uncle's estate was worth about a year's salary at Braniff, which was not a lot of money, but it was tax free. A year and a half after we got this windfall, I bought out my mother's share. Subsequently, I participated in the drilling of over one hundred oil and gas wells. Even with my small percentage, it amounted to a pretty good income.

My income from Uncle Bill's estate started out at about $1,000 a month, which was pretty good for those days. As soon as I began receiving the money from my oil and gas interests, I went to the accounting firm that had handled my uncle's estate, and I asked them to show me how to create a set of double-entry books. The accountant set me up with a set of books exactly like the ones they had been keeping for my uncle.

I kept those books up to date for fifty years. Every time I received income, I deposited the check, credited cash, and debited the entity. At the end of each month, I calculated all the credits and debits, and if they didn't balance, I went back and found my error. We were dealing with ten or twelve different oil and gas companies, and there were thirty leasehold interests and over a thousand royalty interests. Double-entry bookkeeping was the only way to ensure I hadn't forgotten anything.

When I transferred my oil and gas investments to my children, I presented that set of double-entry books to the accountant, and he was suitably impressed.

* * *

Four years before I got into the oil and gas business, I started investing in stocks. To prepare, I read the *Wall Street Journal* for six months or more, and I read *Forbes* magazine, the financial journal, before I ever opened an account at Merrill Lynch, Pierce, Fenner, and Beane. That firm has gone through a lot of changes since then, but I'm still with them. Now, of course, it's Merrill Lynch.

I'm aggressive by nature, so for me it made sense to approach investing aggressively. Most people are afraid to take chances. Consequently they fail to take advantage of the tremendous opportunities available in the stock market. "I don't want to get in the stock market," they say. "I might lose my money." Well, hey, it's possible to lose your money, but it's very improbable that you'll lose all of it, and if you invest wisely over a period of time, it's almost certain that you'll benefit. The market has always shown a tendency to go up over a ten- or twenty-year period. If you keep that in mind, you know there's not much risk in long-term investment. I don't think anyone who stayed in the market for thirty years ever lost money. That's the beauty of the free enterprise system.

Tithing and Abundance

Beth and I decided in the first year of our marriage that we would tithe 10 percent of our earnings, no matter how little money we had. At the time I was still in the military, and we had very little, indeed. Even after I began working for Braniff, our earnings were quite modest, but we followed through with our commitment, and later we always gave more than the prescribed 10 percent.

I have to think our tithing led to the inheritance from my uncle, which was completely unexpected. I think God was, once again, doing for me what I could not do for myself. I had turned my back on the oil and gas business back in 1940, when I chose to go into church work instead. And when God led me to flying airplanes, he let me follow my passion, but it was no big moneymaking proposition. Fifteen years later, He intervened again. God knew I would put my new earnings to use in His service, and so the money came flowing in. Lots of money.

Of course I suffered some losses in the stock market, but

some of my stock investments were incredibly successful. My investments in Dr Pepper, Republic Gypsum, and Walmart grew over 90 percent. The profits were more than we needed by far. After only three years of investing, we began to increase our tithing gradually to 60 percent and eventually to more than 75 percent. We put our windfall to work for God. Much of our giving went to our home church, First Baptist in Dallas, and its associated schools and missions. For instance, in 1996, Dallas Baptist University needed a women's dormitory. Beth and I volunteered to give $1 million if the school would raise the other $2 million. More recently, First Baptist Academy needed a new home. We pledged another $1 million toward the construction cost of the new campus, which is slated for completion in 2017.

* * *

In 1965, I met Cameron "Uncle Cam" Townsend, the founder of Wycliffe Bible Translators, which has projects and missions all over the world and is closely linked with JAARS. At that first meeting, I learned about the work he and his team were doing, and I was impressed.

Uncle Cam had traveled to Guatemala in 1917 to sell Spanish Bibles and soon discovered that many of the people spoke Cakchiquel, not Spanish. Instead of selling Bibles the native Guatemalans and many other native peoples all over the world could not read, he set up a school to teach Bible translation. Eventually that school grew into what is now called Wycliffe Bible Translation. They completed the five hundredth translation in 2000, and their goal is to translate the Bible into every language by 2025.

Bible translation is a monumental task, but it's not all Wycliffe does. In addition to making the Bible accessible to people in the remotest parts of the world, they assist with language development, literacy, and other spiritual and physical needs.

As soon as we learned about Uncle Cam's organization, Beth and I wanted to get involved. We felt strongly that Wycliffe deserved our full support. Over the years, Wycliffe received about 30 percent of all our giving and much of our time and energy. I served on the Wycliffe Linguistics Council for twenty years and the Wycliffe Home Council for seven.

At that first meeting in 1965, I asked Uncle Cam how I could help. He put me on a project to provide a Helio Courier to a mission in Colombia. The airplane was ready to go, but it wasn't paid for. With friends and relatives, we raised the required $8,000 to pay it off. Then I was asked to ferry it to Bogota, which got me involved with JAARS. This was the first of my fifteen overseas ferries, which were about evenly divided between South America, Africa, and Southeast Asia. I ferried airplanes for twenty-eight years, and I have worked with JAARS for over fifty years, providing funds and leadership, serving on the board for thirty-nine years and chairing it for thirteen.

The Braniff Flight Museum

Inside or outside the church, any time I heard of a cause or an organization that struck me as worthy, I would look into it and see what we could do. For instance, in 2007 I visited with the people in charge of the Museum of Flight in Dallas. "Why don't you have a Braniff exhibit out here?" I said.

"We've got $8,000 or so toward a Braniff exhibit that the Clipped Bs raised," they said. The Clipped Bs is an organization founded in 1947 for former Braniff flight attendants. "But we need another $90,000 to really have an exhibit that would portray the airline the way it should be portrayed."

"I'll pledge $30,000 if you'll raise the rest," I said.

The director of development asked if I had any ideas about

raising the matching funds. "I know both of my farming buddies would be interested," I said.

She went straight to Glenn Shoop and Jack Morton. I knew Glenn Shoop at Oklahoma University. He came to work for Braniff two or three months before I did. Jack Morton started two or three weeks after I did, and we all got to be fast friends.

Glenn grew up on a farm in western Oklahoma, and he talked Jack and me into investing in farm properties in north Texas, between Justin and Decatur. The development director made a beeline for those two and talked them into giving $30,000 each. That's called encouraging by example.

* * *

This bountiful life of mine began in my grandfather's modest houses in Okemah and Sulphur, Oklahoma. Fatherless and left to find my own way in the world, I could have made plenty of wrong choices. When I think of my father dying drunk and alone in a boarding house, I thank my heavenly Father for sparing me from such a life. I thank Him for the abundance with which He filled the void my father left. I'm not talking about material possessions now. The money is there to be given away. The true abundance in my life is the love I share with my family, my friends, and my partners in the service of God.

MY FAMILY

I had to learn how to smile. Imagine that. As a boy, I lived in a household with little laughter and joy, ruled by my stern grandfather who didn't know the first thing about warmth and affection. My mother and grandmother bowed to his will, which was to raise my sister and me by his rules.

Growing up the way I did, I wasn't good at personal relationships. I never heard my grandmother, my grandfather, or my mother say "I love you" to me or to each other. I knew they did love me, but I never heard the words, and any demonstrations of loving feelings were hard to come by. I had to go outside of my family to learn how to be a loving person. That's just the way it was.

From that dark house in Sulphur, I could see the white-washed clapboard church my mother took us to every Sunday, and there I learned what it meant to be loved. The Scripture says, "See what kind of love the Father has given to us, that we should be called children of God; and so we are" (1 John 3:1). Is it any wonder that I gave my heart and soul to the heavenly

Father at the tender age of ten? He filled me with His love, and through Him, I learned how to be a loving husband, father, and friend. From that day in 1927 forward, I have remained His steadfast servant, and have done my best to be the kind of man He wants me to be.

* * *

Malcolm Ritchie, who was to have been my best man, was a classmate of mine all through pilot training. He had studied psychology before going into the military, and he made a career of it after the war. I admired him greatly, and we remained friends until he died. One day he said to me, "Orville, you're so well adjusted, you're abnormal."

I took that as a compliment, because, by adjusted, I think he meant I accommodate to any situation and am willing to go with the flow, so to speak. That's true about me. I realize that I'm a part of a greater community on Earth, and as such, I have to adapt to have good relationships. It's not all about me. It's about all of us.

In my long life, I have learned that we need to make friends and maintain those friendships, not for what others can do for us, but so we can have a positive influence on their lives. As a Christian, I have tried to live a life that would reflect my belief in the Lord Jesus Christ and the moral standards He set.

MY ADVENTUROUS FAMILY

The family Beth and I created is very different from the one I grew up in. I admit much of the credit goes to her. I had a busy work schedule, but I still regret spending too little time with my children when they were young. I helped them with schoolwork now and then, but I should have been more involved, showing them how to do things, how to make things, how to put things together, how to play. At the time, I thought since I had learned most things on my own, they could too, and that's a pretty narrow-minded attitude. Nevertheless, I like to think Beth and I showed our children how to build strong, loving relationships, and we demonstrated the rewards of living a life of service to God and those less fortunate.

My work as a pilot kept me away from my family a lot, but on the plus side, thanks to Braniff, our children traveled the world at a young age, essentially for free. They experienced different cultures, befriended people of various races and ethnic backgrounds, and saw with their own eyes the wonders of God's creation.

For our first family trip, we took all four kids to Hawaii and spent ten days on Maui. That was a big hit, and we followed up with a vacation in South America. We spent a week in Lima, Peru, and a second week visiting close friends who were serving as missionaries in Brazil. The next year we went on a two-week vacation that took us to Paris, Beirut, and to Kenya and Uganda in East Africa.

The Rogers Family Reunions

Our kids appreciated the family vacations so much that thirty-one years ago, when they all had kids of their own, we instituted an annual family reunion, which often involves major international travel. Together we have experienced the many wonders of this world near and far, including China, Australia, Africa, the Mediterranean, and the Caribbean. In 2015, we stayed closer to home and discovered the many charms of New England. Sixteen years ago we traveled all the way to Antarctica and there, in that strange beauty, we stood in awe of God's creation.

Antarctica

By the time I turned eighty, I had visited most of the places around the world that I wanted to see, but Antarctica remained on my bucket list. I started talking to Beth about taking the family, but she wasn't so sure about that idea.

"Let's you and I go down there and give it a test run," I said.

In December 1999, we flew to Ushuaia in southern Chile and boarded a Norwegian cruise ship carrying one hundred passengers and a ninety-five-member crew. The trip from

Chile to Antarctica took nearly two days, and we spent nine or ten days cruising among the Antarctic Islands, a frozen land as devoid of color as a black and white photograph.

The sea and sky are teeming with life. Seals and whales darken great swathes of the water, and spectacular birds swoop and circle overhead. The wings of one very special bird looked dull brown from below, but when they landed, you saw the tops were dappled with white crosses.

I thought those beautiful creatures were my favorite, but then I met the penguins. We were told not to approach them, and we never did. One day, though, when there was a break in the line of penguins going down to the sea to feed, I bent the rule a little bit. I entered the break in their pathway, and so help me, about three or four of them walked up to me. I could almost have touched them. They stopped and looked up at me as if to say, "What are you doing in my way?" After a few moments they waddled around me and continued on down to the sea.

In Antarctica I experienced God's creation like a child discovering it all for the first time. The place inspired a sense of wonder in me that I hadn't felt since my days flying into the glory, above the clouds, rainbows encircling my vision, the breath of God under my wings.

Beth and I agreed the whole Rogers clan had to experience this incredible place. The next year, the family reunion was in Antarctica. Everyone came except Susan and her girls and two of Rick's boys, who made the trip the following year. The kids and grandkids loved it as much as we did, as much as I knew they would.

Rick and Jane's daughter, Sarah Beth, was not quite four on the Antarctica cruise. The next winter, during a ski lesson in New Mexico, the instructor said, "Honey, have you ever seen snow before?"

"Oh, yes," she said.

"Where?" he asked.

Enunciating perfectly, she said, "In Antarctica."

You could have tipped him over.

Return to Africa

In the summer of 2016, twenty-seven members of my family traveled with me to Kenya and Tanzania. Beth and I had taken our kids to Kenya and Uganda the summer the twins were in third grade. They were probably nine. Susan says that trip changed her life. She's been back twice since then, and this summer she was able to show this awe-inspiring place to her children.

One of the highlights of our trip was a visit to northern Tanzania to see the Ngoro Ngoro crater, a volcanic caldera, twelve miles across, with steep walls that resulted when the volcano died and collapsed in on itself. The rim walls are fairly steep, and the animals that migrated down into the caldera over the centuries remain there and form a sort of microcosm of African wildlife. As a result, Ngoro Ngoro is home to the largest concentration of big game on the continent. I am so thankful that I could show my grandchildren and great-grandchildren one of the most spectacular places on God's earth.

A LEGACY OF SERVICE

One of the things I'm proudest of is the dedication all of my children have to living a life in the service of our Lord. Our son Bill is on the staff of Dallas Baptist University. His area is fundraising, which is challenging and important work. He attended Baylor University and earned a master's degree in business administration, so he has a long history of working in Christian education, and I am very proud of him for that. In fact, I'm very proud of all my kids and their mates.

James Richard, who we call Rick, is a pediatrician in Tyler, Texas. It's kind of funny—he married a nurse, and his twin, Susan, is a nurse married to a doctor. The twins have been very close all of their lives. I guess that's normal. They lived in separate towns for about ten years, when Susan's husband, Ken Eveland, completed his residency in general surgery and took a position in Moses Lake, Washington. But they reunited when Ken had an opportunity to go to work with the University of Texas Health Science Center at Tyler.

In the summer of 1983, after Rick's rotation in pediatrics, Rick and Jane spent seven months at a remote mission in Benin, West Africa. They traveled with their two young children—two-year-old Curtis and two-month-old Steven—and that was difficult, but they knew it would be many years before Rick gained enough seniority in a medical practice to merit a leave of absence.

Before the mission trip, Rick had investigated the potential for joining a practice in Tyler and found a pediatrician in a solo practice who wanted help. Rick interviewed with him, and the young doctor said he would accept Rick as a partner if he would agree to join him directly out of his rotation.

"I'm going to go on a medical mission trip before I settle into a practice," Rick said. "I feel it's my calling."

"Sorry," the doctor said. "I can't wait for you."

As He did for me so many times, God intervened. When Rick and Jane returned from Africa seven months later, the position hadn't been filled. Of course, Rick accepted the offer.

This is the way God works. I experienced His loving attention to every detail of my own life, and I see His presence in the lives of my children. Rick sacrificed the assurance of the practice he really wanted in order to serve God in Africa first, and God rewarded him beyond anything that Rick could have created by himself. Rick joined the practice, and less than three years later, the pediatrician decided to quit. He sold his building and his practice to Rick.

Rick was on his own in Tyler Pediatrics for three or four years before he started adding other doctors to the practice, one every year or two until he had four or five partners. Eventually CHRISTUS Trinity Mother Frances hospital in Tyler bought the building and the practice. The new arrangement enables Rick to devote more time to missionary work, which is his abiding passion.

Rick and Jane are very active in Young Life, a youth-oriented evangelistic organization that operates all over the world. Rick likes to travel, and through Young Life he has taken groups to West Africa, Kenya, and Tanzania many times. At the end of each youth group's visit, he leads a climb of Mount Kilimanjaro.

Ken and Susan continue to live in Tyler, but Ken retired from the UT Health Science Center at Tyler in 2005 to devote himself to medical missions full time. He's an officer on the board of Refuge International, an organization headquartered in Longview, Texas, that focuses on medical missions in Guatemala. He recruits doctors and trains them for the mission trips; he goes down there himself eight to twelve times a year for one or two weeks at a time. Susan often goes with him and serves as a nurse.

I do not think it is a coincidence that all three of my children devote themselves so vigorously to doing God's work and spreading His word. As they grew up, they saw firsthand the power of God's love in our family and the rich rewards of living in His service.

Guatemala Mission

When I was ninety-three years old, and two years later, at ninety-five, I went on a medical mission trip to Guatemala with Refuge International. They have four locations in Guatemala—Petén, Chocola, Sarstun, and San Raymundo, which is about an hour north of Guatemala City. The medical teams they recruit travel to these locations several times a year for eight days at a time.

Rick; Jane; their daughter, Sarah Beth, who was eleven years old at the time; and Susan accompanied me on my first trip in February 2009. Ken was already there. He usually goes down a day early to organize the prescription and over-the-counter medications for the pharmacy volunteers.

The rest of us arrived in San Raymundo on a Saturday and spent the evening getting organized. In addition to Ken, serving as general surgeon, there were two orthopedic surgeons on that trip. Rick was the pediatrician. Susan and Jane served as nurses, and Sarah Beth and I were assigned to the pharmacy.

When the doors opened Sunday morning at seven or eight o'clock, the patients were already lined up fifty deep. We stayed open until at least six o'clock each night, sometimes later. The work never stopped. The team members, which included three nurses in addition to Jane and Susan and sixteen nurses-in-training, took turns breaking for lunch, so patients were treated all day long without interruption.

The clinic pharmacy is stocked with a limited selection of medications donated by hospitals or clinics in the US as there are no local pharmacies to call upon. I guess if you're wealthy enough, you have access to medications in Guatemala, but for most people the cost is prohibitive.

Sarah Beth and I had the privilege of dispensing medications. We probably served a hundred people a day. The founder of Refuge International, Deborah Bell, is an Certified Family Nurse Practitioner experienced in pharmacology. She checks out every medication that is handed out and works tirelessly, making sure everyone is well taken care of.

The surgeons see fifty to sixty patients during the week. Sometimes they have two sections in the operating room, which enables them to do two surgeries at the same time. During that trip, the surgical patients were released to Susan, who took charge of the post-op nurses in the recovery room. Most of the surgeries, perhaps half, were hernias. They had a few Ob-gyn cases, and one or two babies were delivered during the week.

On Sunday morning, a man in his late thirties or early

forties came to see a doctor. His leg was just dangling like a puppet's with a broken string. He had been in an automobile accident about a year before and suffered a broken leg. The Guatemalan doctors set his leg and put an eight-inch plate along the shinbone attached with eight screws. At some point, the screws came out, and the plate fell off. After a brief examination at our mission clinic, the orthopedist said, "Sir, there's only one thing we can do to help you, and that's take your leg off."

The man didn't hesitate. "Do it," he said.

Monday morning, the man with the ruined leg came back for his amputation. One of the orthopedic surgeons had gone to a hardware store and purchased a hacksaw. After sterilizing it, they used it to cut the leg off midpoint between the knee and the ankle. He stayed in the post-op area until we left, and it appeared that the operation had been a complete success.

On Friday we packed up and traveled to Antigua, a small city in the highlands of southern Guatemala. During the Spanish colonial era, it was one of the greatest cities between Mexico City and Lima, Peru, but it was virtually destroyed by an earthquake. It's still a beautiful place to visit, and, as we did, the clinic volunteers often stop there for a day to get some R&R before flying home on Sunday.

* * *

It means a great deal to me that our children and grandchildren have continued the tradition of service to which Beth and I committed our lives. Maybe the Lord has kept me around because I so enjoy ministering to other people. I like to think that's a trait my children have inherited. Like Beth and I, Rick, Bill, and Susan, as well as their mates, have always empathized with the underdogs and the underprivileged. For the Rogers clan, it's our ministry.

As a fatherless child, I never dreamed I would be graced with the love of my dear Beth, and that through the two of us, God would create this tribe of wonderful people: my family.

FLYING INTO
THE GLORY

*"Eye hath not seen, nor ear heard, neither have
entered into the heart of man, the things which
God hath prepared for them that love him."*
—1 CORINTHIANS 2:9

God blessed me with the gift of flight, and those hours spent high above the earth brought me joy and an abiding sense of wonder. Flying the Cessna over North Texas and southern Oklahoma, I also gained a fair amount of perspective on God's creation and my place in it.

Whenever I headed south from Dallas, I looked down on Hubbard, where my life began in a rough ranch house outside of town. Flying north, I followed the path my parents took when they moved to Oklahoma. From high over the Great Plains, I could almost see my dad lighting out for California on the old Postal Highway, which, three years later, became Route 66. He probably never dreamed his boy would have bigger, better adventures, would fly across the oceans serving another father, the heavenly Father, who watches over us and loves us and never leaves us.

In my little Cessna, I circled the school in Sulphur, like Lindbergh did that summer of 1927, when he lit the fire in me—the everlasting yearning to fly. From my vantage point, I returned for a moment to my childhood on the Oklahoma plains, knowing that my life had turned out better than I ever imagined, just as God intended.

I passed over OU, where I first met the love of my life, before heading south to Fort Worth, where Beth and I attended Southwestern Baptist Theological Seminary. My flying days had already begun by the time we were there, and God saw to it they would not end for another fifty-seven years.

I often flew over Carswell Air Force Base, the SAC air base where I was stationed, and thought about the thrill of flying that B-36, the world's biggest airplane at the time. Sometimes, just for a moment, I would relive the mixed emotions I experienced carrying a dummy bomb during those practice missions, praying I would never have to drop a real atomic bomb over Moscow.

During these meanders over North Texas, I flew over Love Field, site of thousands of take-offs and landings for Braniff. I surveyed my farm properties up by Justin to see how they were surviving the latest drought, maybe check the fences.

Taking a quick aerial tour of downtown Dallas, I could see the tall steeple of the First Baptist Church, where my children were baptized, and where I have served as a deacon since 1953. A quick turn over White Rock Lake took me back to the years of running around and around it, grateful for the tremendous strength and endurance God granted me.

In all those flights, I took the greatest pleasure in seeing the life Beth and I built together. As I flew low over the trees and our beautiful home by the lake, I reached back through the decades and saw our kids playing in the meadows, growing up happy and healthy and secure in our large, loving family.

For sixty-four years, nine months, and five days, Beth and I shared this great adventure. I thank God every day for all the good that flows from our blessed union and for the abundance He has bestowed on me.

Epilogue

September 19, 2013

My Dear Children,

I would like to tell you about a dream I had recently—and I need to write it down to cement it in my memory.

For a long time now, I have been wondering why I could never dream about my wife, the one who had been so near and dear to me for seventy years or so. I had dreamed about friends and loved ones. So some time back I began to ask God for that kind of dream.

A few nights ago I had this very vivid dream about her. We were in a room together, though I did not notice the surroundings. She was seated on pedestal, though I could not see it. She was dressed in a white flowing garment. (Do I dare interpret the pedestal as being where I had placed her all our life together, and the white as the purity with which I had always viewed her?) As I walked up closer to her, almost within touching range, she looked at me, half smiling, and our eyes locked for a few seconds. An intense feeling came over me that we were sharing our thoughts together, realizing the deep love we had for one another, and remembering the wonderful experiences of life together. We did not share a word, although I felt we were expressing our thoughts to each other, and reaffirming our love for each other. There, it ends.

Your loving Dad

THE ROGERS FAMILY

Orville Curtis, Jr. (died November 18, 1970)
William (Bill)
    m. Melanie
        Shannon
            m. Patrick McCrory
                Evie, Ellie, Lillie
        Elizabeth
            m. Brad Thurman
                Ryan, Will, Bradley
Richard (Rick)
    m. Jane
        Curtis
        Steven
        Will
        Michael
            m. Nina
        Sarah Beth
Susan
    m. Kenneth Eveland
        Jennifer
            m. Chris McGuirk
                Madison, Caleb, Hunter
        Jessica
            m. Neal Anthony
                Esther
                Hallie